WRESTLING WITH

DESTINY

·

·

·

·

A Layman Searches for Joy, Purpose & Fruitfulness

WRESTLING WITH DESTINY
A Layman Searches for Joy, Purpose & Fruitfulness

Printed in the United States of America

Published by *Faranhyll* P R E S S
P.O. Box 2193, Glenwood Springs, Colorado 81602

ISBN 978-0-9774078-0-4 and 0-9774078-0-2

WRESTLING WITH
DESTINY

.
.
.
.

A Layman Searches for Joy, Purpose & Fruitfulness

.
.
.

BILL WILLIAMS
Workbook by Kathy Williams

Faranhyll PRESS

TABLE OF CONTENTS

TABLE OF CONTENTS

TABLE OF CONTENTS

TABLE OF CONTENTS

TABLE OF CONTENTS

PREFACE

The reader might wonder what prompted the writing of this book. Kathy and I asked ourselves that same question and needed to answer it to our satisfaction before we undertook the immense effort. We came to three conclusions that were sufficient to energize the task.

The first and most powerful answer is actually one of the principles discussed in the book—we were compelled to. We could not get past an incredible urge to put our thoughts and experiences on paper regarding this mysterious subject of destiny, even if it seemed a sophomoric, unsophisticated treatment of the subject.

Secondly, we wanted to give to Jesus Christ a love offering that He might use in the development of His Kingdom. Hopefully this book will draw readers into a closer, more intimate relationship with their Creator.

The Apostle Peter expressed our yearning best when he said: "Above all, keep fervent in your love for one another, because love covers a multitude of sins." I say this because I am deeply appreciative of how God has dealt with me in my sinfulness. I have often been wayward, yet He has always forgiven me and patiently guided me back to the right way. At times His discipline has been stern. But He has always been there and never abandoned me. The long suffering love of God is truly an amazing thing. This book is a small way I can say thank you to Jesus for loving me and not giving up on me.

And lastly, we have a deep affection and concern for lay people that they might find joy, purpose and fruitfulness in their lives. They are our brothers and sisters, and we are one with them. By God's grace, we have come to love, as Charles Spurgeon said, "the deliciousness of work" more than play. But that blessing came with a marvelous struggle, a wrestling of sorts, trying to extract meaning and a sense of destiny from our obscure existence. Our hearts desire is that this book will help lay people love their work more than play and recognize that their work is important and centered in a wondrous relationship with Jesus Christ that will endure forever.

I have chosen to primarily tell stories as my methodology for sharing the concepts presented in the book. I have drawn from my life, the lives of family members, acquaintances, and historical figures. The personal examples do not appear in chronological order, but rather as they relate to the particular topics.

Seneca, the Roman philosopher, said: "The day thou fearest as the last is the birthday of eternity." We are convinced of the love and good purposes of God regarding eternity. We believe that people are the most important thing in life and that our lives count for something in His eternal plan. May God use our humble effort to influence many lives in light of these truths.

SECTION ONE
Looking Backward, Inward, and Upward

We need a starting place if we are to understand God's purposes for our lives. That starting place is to look backward, over our shoulders if you will, at our past. We have all been impacted by our past.

Then we need to look inward to our hearts and think about the influence the past has had on us. An analysis of our personal histories reveals the source of our beliefs and values. They are the foundation upon which we are building our lives. Is that foundation trustworthy or faulty? If we continue to live our lives on the foundation of our existing beliefs and values, will it lead to a life of joy, purpose and fruitfulness, or calamity? Perhaps change is warranted in some areas of our lives.

Then we need to look upward and think about God's values as revealed in the Bible. What has He promised to reward in eternity? If we align our beliefs and values with God's, we then have a solid foundation that will lead to a promising future, one of joy, purpose and fruitfulness.

•   •   •   •

"Because it is our nature as humans that for true achievement, emotional fulfilment and spiritual attainment, we need higher intensity of purpose than everyday concerns can provide."

—Phillip Dimitrov
Former Prime Minister, Bulgaria

CHAPTER ONE
A Quest for Purpose: A Pilgrimage Begins

1
Born in a Young Boy's Heart

December 2, 1996, was a sunny, crisply cold day in southwest Missouri. Unfortunately, I was in a funeral procession slowly winding its way up a hill to a small town's cemetery. I was going to bury one of the most important people in my life—my father. My emotions had been battered by the loss. I remember as a teenager once getting caught in a rainstorm as I rode my motorcycle. The raindrops were extremely painful as they pelted me. It felt like being pricked by needles all over my body. That's the way the loss of my father felt, only I was being pelted and pricked on the inside.

I always thought the cemetery had a tranquil setting. It sits on a small hill and is covered with large oak trees. From there you see a panorama of the rolling, mid-western countryside. The grave markers date back to pre-Civil War days when the town was first settled.

How did such an obscure place come to play such an important role in my life, I pondered. My mind flashed back to my long history with the cemetery.

It started on a summer day in 1954. I was a freckle-faced boy riding my bike to the town park to swim with my pals when I saw a stream of cars driving up what the locals call Cemetery Hill. I peddled up the hill, hid behind one of the stately oaks and watched the procession from a safe distance.

After everyone left, I mustered the courage to go to the gravesite. I was curious to see what would happen next. It was exciting and frightening at the same time.

I can still picture the two crusty old gravediggers in their coveralls talking and chewing tobacco. Though nervous, I asked if I could watch, and they said yes.

I remember distinctly how I felt about them. It was the same way I felt about Captain Hook from the original animated version of

Peter Pan. In my young mind, Captain Hook was the personification of evil, and so were they.

The indifference to their task was disturbing, as they casually shoveled dirt on the coffin. They weren't being irreverent, but they certainly were nonchalant. Their work seemed so inconsequential to them.

They were like most of the old men in town. It was interesting to ride my bike to the town gazebo, sit on the steps and listen to the old-timers. They all looked the same, as if conforming to a mandatory dress code. They were in coveralls, unshaven and smoking or chewing tobacco. They would sit all day whittling, swearing and recalling stories of World War I, The Great Depression or World War II.

All this behavior created questions in my mind about what a man should be. I wondered if that's what I'd be like as a man. It seemed to me that manhood should be something different. However, this was their idea of a grand retirement, because they weren't in the sawmills or coal mines doing backbreaking labor anymore.

I sensed that it was just a matter of time till those gravediggers would be regulars at the gazebo. The combination of their persona, their indifference to their work and my realization that there was actually a body inside that coffin made my time by the grave a fascinating yet terrifying moment.

My young mind raced with all kinds of new questions, things I'd not thought about before. I wondered about life and death, what would happen to that body, will this happen to me and on and on. I remember trying to avoid the cemetery after that. It scared me. It had become a creepy, macabre place.

I was much affected by this, so much so that I had a hard time sleeping after the incident. My grandmother's bedroom had a large wardrobe closet reminiscent of C.S. Lewis' *The Lion, The Witch, and The Wardrobe*. At night, the moonlight shining through the windows cast shadows of the wardrobe on the wall. I was sure they were really ghosts watching me, waiting for me to doze off so they could get me.

The fear and sleeplessness went on for several weeks. Then I experienced what to me was a true miracle. My aunt had given me a children's pictorial Bible. One night at bedtime, my Mom read me a few of the stories, and, to my surprise, I didn't have any nightmares. I associated my good night's sleep with the Bible. It was magic.

After that, I got another copy of the Bible, a small pocket sized version. This became a good luck charm for me—a spiritualized version of a rabbit's foot. I secretly carried it with me everywhere. First, it was hidden in the saddlebag of my bike. As I grew older, it migrated to the storage compartment of my motorcycle and eventually came to rest in the glove compartment of my first car.

To me there was something mysterious and powerful about the Bible, only I didn't know what it was. But it had chased the ghosts away, and I was going to have it close by always.

We're all on a spiritual pilgrimage, and I've concluded that developing an experiential knowledge of Jesus Christ is a process consisting of numerous events. That was the start of the process for me. What really happened to me that day in 1954 at the cemetery that impacted me in such a powerful way? I certainly couldn't articulate it at the time. In retrospect, I believe it was my first inkling of the brevity, gravity and finality of life—and it jolted me.

My next encounter with the cemetery came in 1956. Only this time it involved my own family. We were burying my grandfather.

Years elapsed before I had to return to the cemetery. The next trip occurred in 1981. By then I was a young man finding my way in the world. This time we were laying to rest my beloved grandmother, a woman who had been fundamental to my development and a true blessing to me.

That was my last encounter with Cemetery Hill until I returned on that frosty December morning in 1996—a trip which proved to be the toughest of them all. Dad had been wonderful—a friend, mentor and confidant. One couldn't ask for more in a father. Still reeling from the eulogy I had just delivered, I was filled with a bizarre combination of adrenalin, sadness and relief.

Losing a parent triggered emotions I'd never felt before. It's as if his life had been a barrier against death, shielding me from my own mortality. But now that barrier was gone, and I felt alone and exposed.

Cancer had taken his life. He was incredibly gallant in the midst of his suffering, handling his trial with grace and dignity. He never complained and was determined to face death in a way that gave his family a positive model of a man walking through the "valley of the shadow of death" [3] with the God he had learned to trust.

2

Reflections

Over the years, the cemetery has become an increasingly important place to me. I go to pay respect to my family members but also to ponder my destiny, my ultimate reality—the fabric and meaning of my life.

It was a scary place as a boy, but now it's a convicting and sobering place. When I'm there, I sense the finality of death, as I look at the grave markers of the people I love so much. Gone forever is their opportunity to affect their destinies. Their earthly lives are finished—completed works.

Those generations are gone. My generation is next. It sobers me to think this will happen to me. I desperately want to make the most of my opportunity to live purposefully and fruitfully. I'm consumed by the realization that one day it will be my turn to die, and my sons will come and weep over me, pondering the meaning of my life and, by implication, theirs.

But beyond that, the cemetery has become a place where I can think, reflect and adjust my perspective. Things seem clearer as I evaluate the calling, purpose and progress of my life when I stand on the site that will mark the end of my earthly pilgrimage.

Cemetery Hill is in Pierce City, Missouri. The little town reminds me of Whistle Stop, the place that served as the setting for the movie, *Fried Green Tomatoes*. Unfortunately, Pierce City dominated the national media in May of 2003, when it was destroyed by a powerful tornado. By God's grace, the little country cemetery was spared.

Gone, however, are the precious shrines of my boyhood. I especially miss my grandparents' home, the site of so much love and childhood adventures. Most of the good memories from my youth happened there.

I went there shortly after the tornado struck. I had to see for my-self and couldn't believe the devastation. What had been my grand-parents' home was now a pile of gnarled trees, hunks of concrete and splintered wood. My heart ached as I observed the destruction.

What caused the pain? What was I longing for? Maybe it was the excitement of rushing out to their hen house to see if the chickens had provided breakfast for us. Or maybe it was those evening walks we took to pick sassafras roots along a nearby spring. Then we'd go back to the house and make sassafras tea. Maybe it was the porch swing where we sat most every night talking about anything that crossed a rambunctious little boy's mind. Certainly, it was the perva-sive sense of peace and well-being that I always felt there.

I also missed the sound of the trains that passed close to their home every evening. The house was so close to the tracks that I would feel the bed shake slightly when they went by. There was something soothing and mysterious about the sound of the whistles blowing. My young mind would be filled with wonder at what laid beyond those tracks. I had a youthful version of wanderlust, curious to find out what was out there. To this day it's difficult for me to hear the sound of a train and not be transported in my mind back to those carefree days.

I couldn't think about the trains without also remembering the hobos. From the Great Depression through the war years they "rode the rails." There was a large cave near my grandparents' home, and the hobos would jump from the trains and live in this cave as they were passing through. It was adventurous to sneak down there and find one or more of them warming themselves by a campfire.

When my grandmother found out I was doing this, she didn't make me stop. Instead, she'd make sandwiches for me to give to them. Needless to say, that made me a big hit with the hobos. Perhaps she did this because she remembered the joblessness of The Depression that first fueled the supply of hobos. She talked about those difficult times often. But, mostly, she did it because she was kind.

This was all very "Tom Sawyer and Huckleberry Finnish" to me. I didn't see them as bums at all. To me they were great adventurers. They got to ride those trains. We'd sit by the fire, and they'd fill my head with stories of what it was like beyond Pierce City in the world I was yearning to see. It seemed they hadn't a care in the world. Their lives seemed exciting.

Those experiences are distant, fond memories existing only in my heart—yet another powerful reminder of the brevity of life. It strikes me that little boys don't have the capacity to either ponder or articulate the meaning of something as profound as destiny. Yet, something happened inside me when I had my first encounter at the cemetery years ago.

Looking back, I think I can verbalize what was birthed in me that day, when I watched the dirt crash down on the first coffin I'd ever seen, covering it with such eerie permanence. It was the realization that someday the dirt would be falling on my coffin and that I desperately wanted to find my purpose in life and experience the satisfaction of having fulfilled it. When that moment comes I want to know that I did not live in vain.

It was the birth of a pilgrimage, as expressed succinctly by the Psalmist: "So teach us to number our days, that we may present to You a heart of wisdom...And do confirm for us the work of our hands; yes, confirm the work of our hands." [4]

3
Childhood Influences Shape Perspective

We are marked by our upbringing in profound ways. Various people and experiences certainly shaped my convictions regarding life. The values that were formed drove me down certain paths, both right and wrong ones. Those experiences and relationships were, in essence, making me me. They branded me in a way as unique as my genetic code. Those experiences and relationships formed my circumstantial genealogy, the roadmap of my values, showing me how I came to view life.

Some aspects of my circumstantial genealogy loom large in my thinking. Children have such sensitive spirits. I didn't understand a lot of what I witnessed. But I sensed when something was right or wrong, as I watched friends and relatives live frustrated, unfulfilled lives.

How come it hurt so much when relatives argued? Something seemed extremely wrong when that occurred. Unfortunately, there was often arguing in our family. I always found it unsettling, disturbing my sense of safety and well-being. It created feelings of insecurity.

How come none of the families in my neighborhood seemed to have homes that were havens of safety and security? I remember my friend Carl's home. I can still picture his dad sitting in his easy chair under a lamp in an otherwise poorly lit room, a cigarette in one hand and a beer in the other. He drank a six-pack of beer most every night and often beat my friend. I always wished that I could have been big enough to defend Carl. By the time I was, his dad had died from the effects of alcoholism.

How come when we had BBQs in the neighborhood all the fathers ever seemed to do was complain about their jobs and criticize their bosses? Their unhappiness was obvious. Work I thought must be a bad thing, something to be avoided. I hoped my life would not be marked by such things.

This was further compounded by my own experience with work as a child. Essentially, I lost a large part of my childhood working in my family's franchise fast food restaurant. Although my parents loved me, they innocently violated about every child labor law that ever existed. However, there was no choice. My dad's venture as an entrepreneur didn't work well. We all had to work long hours just to get by. I would go to school and then catch a bus out to the restaurant, roughly ten miles away. I'd work there till about midnight and then ride home with one of my parents.

Summers were even worse. The restaurant was open from 11:00 AM till 11:00 PM, so we were putting in routine fourteen-hour days. That was life most every day from the time I was seven until I was fifteen.

The highlight of my life during those unpleasant years was my little league baseball team. I got off Wednesday evenings for practice and Sunday afternoons for our weekly game. I lived for Sunday afternoons. They never lasted long enough.

For several years, there was no Christmas. The first day back at school after the holidays was always torture. Everyone had on their new clothes and talked about what they'd gotten for Christmas. I didn't have anything to talk about, so I tried to be inconspicuous. Nonetheless, those times were humiliating.

This experience marked me deeply, affecting my ideas about work, money and social status. Some of these attitudes were good, but some I am still trying to change forty years later. It left me bent on finding something to do that I could enjoy and not despise. I was driven to be wealthy and to never again experience the poverty we had known. It made me determined to be successful, to do something with my life. I craved respect.

The character development created by working in the restaurant all those years was a positive thing, but it left me more serious and intense than others my age. My friends to this day tease me about my intensity.

4
What's So Special about a Knife and Fork?

The one person who positively stood out was my grandmother. I cherished her. The world has no knowledge of her, yet, to me, she was a woman of real importance. She influenced me greatly, stimulating my perspective on God, family, love and work.

There was a special bond between us. I loved being with her. It felt good being in her home, even though I didn't completely understand why. Years later, I realized this was the atmosphere I craved for in my own home. Somehow I wanted my life to be like hers, and I wanted to marry someone who had the values and quality of life she had.

She died in 1981 at the age of eighty-five, and I delivered her eulogy. Somehow, I've always been the designated family eulogist, a position I don't particularly relish. Even on her deathbed, she called out for me, and I regretted not being there to comfort her.

She was very poor and had few possessions. I asked for two seemingly insignificant items from her personal effects—what my family affectionately calls "the little knife and fork." I say "seemingly insignificant," but, in reality, these two utensils were symbols of her values and the spiritual truths that marked her life.

When visiting, I would often find her in the kitchen making apple dumplings or pumpkin pie—my two favorites. I would rush into her arms, give her a big hug and kiss, then jump up on a high stool and watch her cook.

We would talk as she cooked. For some reason, she really enjoyed me, probably a natural reaction of her grandmother's heart. Regardless, it made me feel good about myself. It's always comforting to be around someone if you know they love you. It was easy for me to make her laugh. I guess because kids say such silly things. But I thought it was because I was a witty person. At any rate, her laughter was positive reinforcement for me.

Then came the special moment—the first bite. For this I got to use her "little knife and fork."

Those utensils always intrigued me. The knife was small with the blade almost worn away from use. She had covered the wooden handle with black electrical tape to keep it from falling apart. The small fork was all metal, dark and tarnished. It had two thin prongs worn down by use. We were always amazed that she continued to use these utensils, but she did till the day she died.

After her funeral, Dad gave me the "little knife and fork" and told me the story about how she had acquired these two heirlooms, a story which I had never heard.

It was during the Great Depression when my dad was a boy. The only work my grandfather could find during those difficult times was hauling garbage from hotels in Joplin, Missouri, out to nearby pig farms. Times were desperate, and my grandmother, always the frugal one, would sift through the garbage to see if there was anything she could salvage before giving the scraps to the pigs. That's where she found the "little knife and fork." The hotel had thrown them away because they were worn out, but my grandmother used them for fifty-five more years.

How could these old kitchen utensils capture the essence of a woman's life? To me they represented so many things: love, family life, simplicity, servanthood and good stewardship. Never did a person get more out of less than she, and all the while without complaining or coveting new things. Her life was uncomplicated and frugal.

Secondly, I sensed that a purposeful life might not be equated with material success. She used those implements to create an atmosphere of love and joy. I realize now how desperately poor my grandparents had been. Their home was by the railroad tracks, but it was on the wrong side. Yet, she always seemed happy. Her poverty was different from mine. It didn't affect her like my poverty affected me. I was driven to overcome this situation, but she never was.

She exuded love and contentment. I came to understand that her joy came from knowing Jesus Christ and from serving those around her.

Today the "little knife and fork" are mounted and have a place of honor in my office. I look at them often and am reminded that I need to try to follow her example.

5
An Intimidating Word!

Was my grandmother a woman of destiny, or was she a simple countrywoman whose life was of little importance?

The New American Standard Bible uses the words destine, destined, and destiny thirteen times. It's a very big word, broad in scope and hard to understand. It can be a frightening word and is subject to much misinterpretation.

After all, Abraham Lincoln and Winston Churchill were "men of destiny." But is that true of us lay people? Isn't destiny a fatalistic thing that cannot be altered? What if I miss mine? These are all troubling thoughts.

In the Bible, destiny literally means *appointment*. God has ordained appointments for us in life. All of our collective appointments make a life, or a destiny, if you will.

Appointments are the daily circumstances of our lives. They require responses from us. They are always opportunities to grow spiritually, if we will respond to them appropriately. Our appropriate responses build a platform that prepares us for future appointments.

Appointments can be for a few seconds or for many years. Choosing to not participate in an argument takes only a few seconds. Other appointments like a career or a marriage last for years.

Appointments always affect our character. Our responses define who we are becoming. They prepare us for our roles in life, what we are called to do and what our eventual life's message will be.

Appointments aren't always understood when we encounter them but are often understood in retrospect. For instance, some of my appointments in life have involved leadership. Yet many of my earlier appointments involved working for difficult people. God used those appointments to teach me about submission to authority, something I wasn't very good at, but needed to learn if I was ever to be a good leader. It was through those painful appointments that I learned about how to handle authority more wisely. I seldom understood the lessons when I actually lived the early appointments but later came to appreciate the value of those experiences.

When we view our appointments with God's perspective, our probability of finding joy, purpose and fruitfulness in life is greatly enhanced.

One of my grandmother's appointments was to plant spiritual seeds into a mischievous little boy's heart. Can such a simple thing be relevant in the context of a subject as vast as destiny?

As a result of the impact of her life, I've concluded something about destiny. We often make the mistake of looking for that grandiose calling, but in reality a significant destiny can be achieved by responding to the circumstances of life with grace, love and obedience.

Part of obedience is to trust God to use our responses for His purposes, which we might not understand till we get to eternity. That's what my grandmother did.

John Lennon said: "Life is what happens to you while you're busy making other plans." I agree.

If loving a little boy was a God-ordained appointment for her, my grandmother kept it well. She may have appeared to be an insignificant person, but she was important to me.

An obedient life bears fruit even after the person is gone. The impact of her existence lives on through the many things she ingrained in me. As Jesus told His disciples, "…but I chose you, and appointed you, that you should go and bear fruit, and that your fruit should remain." [5]

6

Books and Finding Purpose

Reading biographies exerted a powerful influence on me and fueled my curiosity about my purpose in life. It still does. Books have been some of my best friends, and the people I read about have been my mentors. They never argued with me, criticized me or told me what to do. They gave me their lives to observe, and let me draw my own conclusions.

Os Guinness in *The Call* said: "Real lives touch us profoundly— they stir, challenge, rebuke, shame, amuse, and inspire at levels of which we are hardly aware. That is why biographies are the literature of calling; few things are less mechanical." [6]

I fondly remember rainy days when I would open my bedroom window far enough to feel a slight mist and read away an otherwise dreary, mid-western day. I would be transported to a far away time and place and observe a famous person's life evolve.

Biographies were intriguing because they disclosed various pathways to discover calling, purpose and satisfaction in life. How did events influence people? How were their convictions and skills developed? How did they come to understand their mission in life? Did there seem to be divine guidance and intervention? Were there any patterns that consistently appeared in the lives of different people?

God is mysteriously creative. His work cannot be reduced to a formula. Anne Lamott observed in *Traveling Mercies*: "Life does not seem to present itself to me for my convenience, to box itself up nicely so I can write about it with wisdom and a point to make before putting it on a shelf somewhere. Now, in my early forties, I understand just enough about life to understand that I do not understand much of anything." [7]

The Apostle Paul alluded to this truth when referring to his own salvation and his appointments in life. He said: "But when it pleased God, who separated me from my mother's womb and called me through His grace, to reveal His Son in me, that I might preach Him among the gentiles." [8]

The statements "when it pleased God" and "to reveal His Son in me" are subjective, mysterious things controlled by God. If they were easy to comprehend, then living by faith wouldn't mean much. The initiative lies with God. His callings and revelations are different for everyone. They are like snowflakes. No two are the same.

God's leading is a mystery as it relates to our destinies. Nonetheless, He gives us glimpses of insight, so we can make decisions and navigate our way. That was the value of reading. It revealed principles that seemed to be true of life. I wondered if and when they would apply to mine.

My reading often left me amazed at how many historical figures were unhappy and never understood their purpose. Many ended life poorly, even after great accomplishments. Beethoven died bitter and angry. Mozart died destitute and was buried in an unmarked pauper's grave. The explorer Merewether Lewis committed suicide. Sir Winston Churchill's words toward the end were: "I'm so bored with it all." [9]

Mark Twain's sentiments on this subject were reflected in his autobiography when he wrote: "The burden of pain, care, misery grows heavier year by year. At length ambition is dead, pride is dead, vanity is dead, longing for release is in their place. It comes at last—the only unpoisoned gift earth ever had for them—and they vanish from a world where they were of no consequence; where they achieved nothing; where they were a mistake and a failure and a foolishness." [10]

These were people who profoundly marked the world. Yet as I read about their lives, it seemed that something was missing and wrong. This troubled me. I wondered how people who accomplished so much could not be happy?

Consequently, biographies created a growing conviction that success, fame and historical relevance in life might not guarantee happiness. There were plenty of examples that validated this observation. It was troubling because I found myself yearning for these distinctions. Could I give myself to something only to be ultimately unfulfilled?

Walt Henrichsen addresses this issue in his devotional book, *Thoughts from the Diary of a Desperate Man.* In his November 12 entry, he says: "Solomon, in Ecclesiastes, runs an experiment. Because he is richly endowed with wealth, power, and a keen intellect, he dedicates himself to the task of seeking purpose, meaning, and significance from them." [11] According to Henrichsen, this verse is the result of Solomon's experiment: "So I hated life, for the work which has been done under the sun was grievous to me: because everything is futility and striving after wind." [12]

What if Solomon was right? If the fruits of wealth, power and a keen intellect wouldn't bring satisfaction, then what would? Reading fueled my curiosity to find the answers to these questions.

7

A Hollow Victory

I had my first serious experience with failure and success as a teenager. In high school I was driven to accomplish something I thought was significant. I coveted the recognition that came with athletic success. This seems so trite now, but forty years ago, during my formative years, it was very important. Then I was a testosterone-filled, insecure teenager, and this was my whole life.

I attended a school that was recognized as one of the best wrestling schools in Missouri. It had produced a number of state champions, but never a state wrestling title. If you were a state champion at my school, you were a "big man on campus."

It started simply enough. I was at wrestling practice one day sitting on the edge of the mat and talking to a past graduate who was home for the Christmas holidays.

He had been a good wrestler with much potential. However, he'd squandered his opportunity, primarily by partying a lot and not committing himself wholeheartedly to the sport. None of the wrestlers respected him, because everyone knew what he could have accomplished, if he had put his mind to it.

That day he seemed humble and contrite. He proceeded to tell me how regretful he was and how badly he felt about his past conduct. But the opportunity was gone forever, and he knew it full well.

I was sincerely moved by his words. To have real ability and to waste it was a prospect that haunted me. It would be one thing to give it your best and fail. Then at least you could have a clear conscience. But to realize that you could achieve something and didn't because of fear or your own lack of character—that was a prospect that concerned me.

As a result of that conversation, I developed a *carpe diem* mentality that's still with me today. Perhaps you recall the scene from the movie *Dead Poets Society*, with Robin Williams. He takes his students to the school's trophy case and reviews the accomplishments of past students. Then he challenges the boys with the fact that this was their moment, their opportunity, and that they needed to *seize the day!*

I went to the State Tournament a few months later. It was my sophomore year, and, as I sat in the bleachers, I set a goal for myself—to wrestle for the state championship as a junior. I really committed myself to this endeavor. It became my religion. 365 days later I was doing exactly that.

However, I never loved wrestling for wrestling's sake. I loved it for what I thought it could do for me. What I coveted that night in the bleachers was all the attention those guys were getting who were out on the mats.

My first love was basketball, but at 5'6", I wasn't enjoying having my shots stuffed by my taller buddies. I also liked football. As a small safety, I was routinely getting "creamed" by 230-pound running backs coming through the line of scrimmage. That wasn't a lot of fun either.

At least with wrestling, I got to compete against somebody my own size. Plus, I seemed to have a knack for it. I wasn't a natural athlete, but I thought, if I applied myself, maybe I could become successful.

I taped a sign on the ceiling in my bedroom. It said, "You're not a state champion yet." It was the first thing I saw in the morning and the last thing I saw at night. I had a one-dimensional life. I never missed a day of conditioning.

Our team won the prized state tournament in my junior year, but I took second place in my weight class. Yes, I was down there wrestling for the championship, but my goal was to be a state champion.

I had failed in a dramatic and humiliating way. I was on the receiving end of what athletes call "a good old fashioned butt-kicking" in front of thousands of people. I couldn't believe it. I had tied my opponent earlier in the season. One of us got a lot better in two months.

Actually, my life wasn't as one-dimensional as it needed to be. I'd allowed myself to get distracted by the beautiful girl I was dating. This lack of single-mindedness compromised my focus and commitment. I had not paid a high enough price.

I recommitted myself to an even more rigorous pursuit of my goal. I moved from being religious about my quest to becoming a zealous fanatic. That started with breaking up with my girlfriend. We hadn't been getting along well, anyway. But I soon had another girl problem to deal with.

As fate, or destiny, would have it, I was assigned an absolutely gorgeous girl to be my biology/zoology lab partner. This arrangement provided a daily dose of flirtation and temptation. I would leave the class exhausted from desire.

I soon started dating my lab partner. I was worried about whether this would, yet again, compromise my commitment to wrestling. However, she proved to be an asset, not a detriment, to my cause. She was totally supportive, never demanding or angry because I wasn't paying enough attention to her. She became my biggest cheerleader.

She still is. We married six years later and have been together for forty years. Kathy is my active collaborator and the author of the workbook that accompanies this book.

My senior year was my last chance to achieve championship status, and it happened. Our team won the state title again, and I won the individual championship in my weight class. For some strange reason, after I received my medal, I just wanted to be alone and reflect on the experience. I crept beneath the bleachers that held several thousand people and stared at the prize.

My mind was flooded with memories of over 800 consecutive workouts, multiple injuries and the rigorous and painful discipline of maintaining my weight. My expectations were out of control. I had totally given myself to this cause. You mean all I get is this lousy medal? It should have been more fulfilling. I kept waiting for this emotional rush of satisfaction, but it never came, not then or the next day or ever. The external reward did not satisfy my internal yearnings.

Apparently Solomon was right. I distinctly remember the frustration realizing that something was still missing. What was it?

8
Accomplishments without God

I attended college on a wrestling scholarship and had some success in the sport, but my heart wasn't in it. The scholarship helped financially, but the main reason I wrestled in college was to meet the expectations of others. When that's your motive, tasks can be burdensome.

I wanted to accomplish something special, but my success with the sport in high school had been frustrating. I had cared so much, and it didn't satisfy. What about the big issues in life—my marriage, career and ultimate purpose? I continued to be anxious about my future.

I felt guilty for being so self-absorbed. Plus, my self-absorption was confusing. As I reflected on that championship, I realized it had been all about me. It was about being popular, accepted and known for something. Those things happened, and I still felt insecure and unfulfilled.

I thought of my grandmother and how God had been the foundation of her life. She didn't have any social status or popularity. In addition, she was extremely poor, yet she was happy. Her life radiated the peace and inner serenity that was eluding me.

What was the difference between us? The main thing I observed was that she lived serving others. I lived serving myself. Her motivations apparently came from a different place than mine.

Even though I wasn't interested in spirituality at the time, I began to believe that there must be a spiritual link to purposeful living. Taking the state championship had been a big accomplishment for me, but it was about self-glorification. There was nothing spiritual about it. I suspected I was looking for happiness in the wrong places.

There were other accomplishments in college, mostly related to my fraternity and student-body activities. Plus, like most students, college was a time of partying. I kept up a good façade. But in my heart, I wasn't happy. It was more of the same frustrations only in a different arena.

I knew I needed to adjust my expectations for the future. I began wrestling with spirituality, or rather the lack of it in my life.

The issue boiled down to one basic but incredibly important question. What would be the foundation I would build my life upon? I was anxious for the answer.

That's when I began to actually read my small good-luck charm Bible, instead of just carrying it around with me. However, I did this quite secretly, wanting to avoid any ridicule from my fraternity brothers.

I found several statements, which succinctly captured the essence of my yearning. I read about the Jewish patriarch Abraham of whom it was said: "He breathed his last and died in a ripe old age, an old man, and satisfied with life." [13] I also liked what the Bible said about King David, who "…after he had served the purpose of God in his own generation, fell asleep, and was laid among his fathers…" [14]

I craved Abraham's satisfaction with life and longed to live a life of purpose like David. Satisfaction and purpose weren't things I was experiencing. To have a life marked by such attributes would be a real accomplishment.

9
An Appointment with God

Then, as destiny would have it, while these spiritual musings were floating around in my head unbeknownst to anyone but God, I came into contact with Campus Crusade for Christ. Their representatives came to our fraternity house and made a presentation one evening. I sat in the audience listening. Inwardly, I felt an excitement as they talked about the claims of Christ.

At the end of the meeting, I asked their spokesman if we could get together for a Coke at the Student Union and talk privately. The next day we met, and the representative for Campus Crusade challenged me to acknowledge Jesus Christ and invite Him into my life.

I left the meeting pondering his suggestion. I paused at a lovely, tranquil spot under a big oak tree by the university library. I sensed that it was what I needed to do. But I wrestled with issues.

It wasn't a popular decision in the rebellious Sixties, and I wasn't interested in the rejection and ridicule I would receive from my friends.

In addition, I was a little offended. I thought I was a Christian. Who did this guy think he was? I never had any issues with believing in God. But when he talked about a personal relationship with Jesus Christ, I knew I didn't have one.

I had never seen God as a person, a being with emotions, character and personality. I believed in Him but saw God as some sort of cosmic force in the universe. He was distant and detached, not close and personal. If He was a person and if a relationship could be experienced, then maybe this was an approach to life that would work. I had lost confidence in my approach.

At the time, my reasoning was purely fueled by self-interest. I was searching for happiness. But it was a starting point that God honored. I was admitting that my way was wrong. I was plotting my way through life without Him, a state of being the Bible calls "sin."

As I mentioned earlier, we're all on a spiritual pilgrimage. The process that started for me in an obscure cemetery in the Midwest led to me asking Jesus Christ to be my Lord and Savior. That's what happened that day under the big oak tree.

My encounter with Christ that day was later validated by a number of distinct changes I experienced. They convinced me that my encounter was real and that God was clearly not who I thought Him to be.

In the days that followed, I sensed that the divine cosmic force in the universe was truly unique. He was a person. I began to pray and sensed that someone was actually listening. I began by asking forgiveness for impulsively moving through life without His input. I became sensitive to the many things I'd done that I knew were wrong, even though I'd rationalized them as being right. I asked forgiveness for those things, as well.

My desires began to change. I didn't will them to change, they just did. Consequently, my partying ways began to tone down. I never consciously thought all of that was wrong or that I could no longer do fun things. I just lost my appetite for it.

Another new discovery was that I had the ability to walk away from temptation if I chose to do so. This was mysterious to me and also very powerful. This was particularly true with my relationship with girls.

Kathy and I had broken up, although it proved to be a short separation. Then one night at a party, I got into a compromising situation with my date. I was somehow able to walk away from it before things got out of hand. It was as if I had a big brother around secretly keeping an eye on me to bail me out of a tough situation if he needed to. I liked that.

Also, I gradually began to feel peace and contentment. Perhaps that's what eluded me the night under the bleachers. My guilt started to subside. I sensed that I had found what my grandmother possessed. I became more optimistic and felt that, with Jesus Christ, I would be able to enjoy and understand my eventual marriage, career, successes and failures—the essence of who He created me to be. I had absolutely no clue how this would occur but felt that I was building life on the right foundation, a spiritual one.

Another change was a newfound enthusiasm for Christian fellowship. I started going to Bible studies and thought they were more fun than parties. This brought the ridicule from my friends that I'd feared. But the rejection didn't hurt as much as I thought it would, because I was enjoying my new friends.

As I had suspected, my decision came with a price. Although there were several incidents, one particularly stands out. One night my best friend came into my room after one of our Bible studies concluded. He was a committed agnostic and was totally put off with my decision. We had quite a heated conversation during which he accused me of abandoning him and committing intellectual suicide, among other things. He also threatened me, saying our relationship would never be the same. Sadly, he was right.

He had just come from the cleaners and was standing with several freshly pressed shirts slung over his shoulder as he delivered the verbal barrage. He got so angry that he hurled his shirts in disgust and raged out of my room.

I was angry and hurt. I was also worried about the friendship because I really liked the guy. I gathered his shirts together and took them to his room. I tried to soothe the situation over but to no avail. Things were never the same.

As a sidebar comment, many of my fraternity brothers became Christians. It was as if Jesus Christ split that fraternity house down the middle, divided by the issue of belief.

However, the joy I was experiencing from the Bible was more important than any loss of friendship that I incurred. The Bible was actually making sense. Reading the Bible used to be frustrating, like opening one of those instruction manuals that comes with a new gadget. They're printed in three or four languages, so you fumble through it desperately looking for the English section. Reading the Bible slowly became like finding the English section. Things were making sense, and I was enjoying life more.

It was a season of life I'll always cherish. I make it a point to venture back to my old college campus periodically. I sit under the beautiful oak tree and reflect on all that's transpired over the years. It was perhaps the supreme defining moment charting the future direction for every aspect of my life.

10
Recognizing Purpose

As my relationship with Christ progressed, I started to recognize purpose in many things. It soon registered with me that God is very utilitarian in His nature. He wastes nothing. Before, I'd seen so many things simply as intrusions in life, frustrations to be endured or problems to escape from.

For instance, I'd considered my youthful experiences with wrestling and work as futile. Then I began to realize that, while painful at the time, they had created character traits that were now helpful to me. Plus, I recognized that God had used those frustrations to draw me toward Christ.

Also, I realized that, in the past, the basis for my love of reading had been curiosity. However, now it became personal relevance. I began to see personal applications in everything I read. This created a sense of intimacy with God. It felt like He was giving me instruction and guidance for life, uniquely provided for me.

For example, as I studied the life of Moses, it became obvious that many of the appointments in his life were training for his ultimate work. I sensed that God was a personal God, who involved Himself spiritually in the lives of people. I concluded that if God did such things for Moses and others, He would probably do the same for me.

I could identify with Moses. When God told Moses to be His spokesman before Pharaoh, Moses' response was half insecurity and half fear. I knew those feelings.

I often found myself in roles of leadership. In my studies, I saw that any leader of substance, Biblical or historical, went through times of suffering. The central truth is that leadership requires character, and character is forged on the anvil of suffering. God seemed determined to build character in people.

Joseph languished in an Egyptian prison, though wrongly accused. Eventually, God made him the leader of Egypt, second only to Pharaoh.

David fled for years from King Saul, though innocent. God eventually made David King of Israel, and he ruled for forty years.

Franklin Roosevelt suffered the agony of polio. This forged his character and did much to prepare him to be a great leader, guiding the country through perilous times.

Winston Churchill was greatly humiliated when his Dardanelles strategy during World War I led to a significant British defeat. As a result, he was relegated to fifteen years of political exile. However, that exile deepened his character and prepared him for the greatness he demonstrated during World War II.

Although I didn't relish this idea of suffering, I could see its value, nonetheless. We all suffer at some point in our lives. What a tremendous thing to understand your suffering, to be comforted through it and to mature as a result of it—to know that it served a purpose.

Sadly, we have all known people who don't have this perspective. Such people become bitter, angry and cynical. They often blame God for their struggles. These aren't fun people to be around.

I began to sense that I was no longer alone. Big brother was in the neighborhood, and He was going to watch over me. This was the ministry of the Holy Spirit which I didn't understand at the time but felt its reality. I came to understand later that His name in Greek was the word *Paracletos,* meaning "one called along side to help."

This feeling reminded me of an incident when I was about six. I was the proud owner of the best baseball card collection in the neighborhood, coveted by all the other kids. We compared cards, traded them and attached the insignificant ones to the wheels of our bikes with a clothespin. The spokes hit them when the bike wheel turned, and the cards made a cool, fluttering sound.

One day I caught one of my friends stealing some of my cards. There was only one logical thing to do: I beat him up. We happened to be in a park, standing on the edge of a fairly steep hill. During our fight, he fell over the edge with a little help from me. He rolled to the bottom of the hill, got all grass stained and ran off crying. At first I was pretty satisfied with myself, but then I wondered what would happen if word of this got back to my dad. It was a troublesome afternoon.

I got to see Dad's reaction that night at supper. We were sitting in the backyard charcoaling our dinner, when my ex-friend came over, accompanied by his parents. The parents were irate and gave Dad an earful about what a bad kid I was. They asked him what he was going to do about me, as if I needed to be kept on a leash. Dad looked at me calmly and asked what happened. I told him that their son had stolen my cards and that other kids would testify to this fact.

Dad got out of his chair, put his face right in the other father's face, planted his index finger on the guy's chest and backed him out of our yard. All the while he was telling him in no uncertain terms that his kid deserved the beating and that the same thing would happen to him if he ever came to our house again. Then he sat back down, looked at me and said, "Good job, son."

I can still picture the fear in the other father's face. It was obvious that he could sense what I already knew—that my dad was no one to mess with.

I'm not commenting on the rightness or wrongness of how my dad handled the situation. But I am saying that my heart was filled with love and gratitude for him. I sensed I had a protector and an advocate. Even if I did something wrong, he would be there for me. That was the feeling I was getting for God—and I liked it.

11
Wrestling with Destiny

It's been fifty years since I started my pilgrimage discovering my appointments in life. I have reviewed only the fundamentals that have propelled me down this road. I've wanted to provide a flavor for how this fascination was formed in me. However, this was never intended to be an autobiography. If anything, I hope that you'll be challenged to think about what's propelling you down your road.

Having said that, I'll reiterate a few key points before we turn our attention to principles that I've observed and believe are valuable.

First, understanding destiny will always remain a great mystery. It can never be fully understood by man. Proverbs 20:24 is still true. "Man's steps are ordained by the Lord, how then can man understand his way?" [15]

The initiative is with God, and He guides us by His grace. Much as we'd like to have a formula to find our destinies or put God in a box, we cannot. Anne Lamott in *Bird by Bird* implies that although there may be a flickering moment of insight, truth isn't often found on bumper stickers. She goes on to insinuate that it can be easier to "embrace absolutes than to suffer reality. Reality can be unforgivingly complex." [16]

In addressing this point about the complexity and mystery of truth, the late theologian Francis Schaeffer made a distinction between exhaustive truth and true truth. The essence of his teaching was that man can never understand anything exhaustively, only God can. But by His grace, we can understand things well enough to make decisions and adjust our conduct accordingly.

Secondly, I stated that everyone has a personal destiny. We all have our own appointments in life. It's not just for prominent people. True, some are set apart for something totally unique. There's only one Billy Graham. That fact doesn't make his calling better than everyone else's—just unique.

Consequently, our appointments can be greatly misunderstood. As a result, we can always be looking for the "big thing" and miss the significance of something we consider to be mundane. I recalled what a powerful influence my grandmother had been because she simply responded with grace, love and obedience to the daily circumstances of her life.

This principle also applies to those few people whose appointments are in prominent, visible arenas. One time I had the privilege of working with the late Tom Landry, the legendary football coach who led the Dallas Cowboys to two Super Bowl victories. His record for wins still ranks him among the top three coaches in history. We worked for several weeks on a project and then spent several days together carrying it out.

The thing that was impressive about Coach Landry was that he responded to the daily circumstances of life just like my grandmother, with grace, love and obedience. He was deferential, always refocusing a conversation back toward someone else. He seemed genuinely interested in other people and was more eager to listen than to speak. He was humble and approachable. I remember one time we were leaving a hotel, anxious to get to the next event, when a number of fans seeking autographs approached him. I was frustrated, because I was tired, and we were late. I knew he felt the same. However, he was very considerate and graciously accommodated them.

I live in a fairly obscure world, but my world matters just as much to God as Coach Landry's world. Coach Landry had a reputation for being a man of integrity in professional football. God thinks it's just as important that I display that same integrity in my career setting.

Since we are prone to these kinds of mistakes, we can misunderstand our appointments and look at them inappropriately. When we do, we devalue ourselves. Yet, God wastes nothing. Hence, we often don't understand our experiences as they relate to our overall purpose. One of the goals for this book is to help people properly evaluate their experiences and view them with God's perspective.

I think God would love to have a bunch of Tom Landry clones in all the spheres of influence in the world. After having worked with him, I realized he was trying to be a clone of Jesus Christ. He did it in professional football, and my grandmother did it in obscure Pierce City, Missouri. God loves the people in both spheres. Tom's reward won't be any better than my grandmother's just because of the differences in their two settings.

Looking back, I can say that this pilgrimage has been nothing like what I expected. I've realized how absolutely trustworthy God is. He wants what is best for me and knows what is best for me far more than I do. In the beginning I was using Him for self-fulfillment, as if He were some Americanized version of a blessing machine up in the sky whose sole function was to cater to my whims.

Because of His trustworthiness, it's comforting to know that my appointments are always appropriate. They are right on schedule. They have been summoned by Divine decree for my well-being.

Lastly, and most significantly, to attempt to find joy, purpose and fruitfulness apart from a relationship with Christ will prove to be an exercise in futility. Sadly, many people don't believe this, Christian and non-Christian alike. Do you?

It appears that God has placed within us this restlessness that yearns for love and significance. Christian and secular psychologists alike tell us that man's deepest needs are for love and significance. I've concluded that these will not be found in the world and its allurements, but in our spirituality.

12
Perceptions or Misperceptions?

My old college wrestling team has frequent reunions that I attend. These get-togethers are always fun but also full of reminders about the brevity of life.

Three of our original twelve starters are deceased—twenty-five percent of our team is dead! Several others have had serious health issues and, by looking at our bodies, it's obvious that we're far from the graceful, young athletes we were forty years ago.

However, I'm still wrestling with the quest for more joy, purpose and fruitfulness in life. Aren't we all? On sleepless nights, do you ever find yourself laying in bed thinking about such things as your career, a strained relationship, family situations, debts, failures and so on? In essence, are you wondering what your life's about?

I frequently question people about this and always hear variations of the same theme. It sounds something like this: "I believe I was created to accomplish something specific to me. I want to find out what that is and then fulfill it."

Many people I've encountered are frustrated, angry, unfulfilled people because time is slipping by, and they feel they're missing it. Some hate their work. To them it's only a paycheck. These are the people Henry David Thoreau was thinking of in his book, *Walden*, when he wrote: "The mass of men lead lives of quiet desperation." [17]

Other people have become cynical. I've met people who've achieved their dreams, only to find that they were not satisfied. Egos may have been gratified and pleasures fed for a season, but these people didn't seem fulfilled at deeper levels.

Part of the purpose of this book is to shed light on what God values as significant, the things we should pursue that will give our lives joy and purpose. Thankfully, His values are not the same as mankind's values. His idea of living a significant life can be achieved by anyone, if we will commit ourselves to Him and pursue His eternal values.

I am a layman continuing to work at finding joy, purpose and fruitfulness in life. My experiences are common to many people. I have grown up in lower and middle income America. Like most people, I haven't attended marquis schools nor reached the pinnacles of fame. My name won't be recorded in any history book. Do these things make me an insignificant person? I suppose it depends on your perspective. The key question is really whether or not your perspective is right.

Early in life, I'd have concluded that my life would be insignificant unless it was marked by noteworthy accomplishments. I also thought that if a Christian wasn't a vocational Christian worker, then he really wasn't in the game. That person would have to settle for a second-class experience with Christ. Now, I'd say that we're all significant people, especially in God's eyes. And, He doesn't measure significance the same ways we do.

This life-long fascination with the search for joy and purpose has created in me a conviction that one of my appointments in life is to share principles and insights that we've discovered along the way.

Abraham Lincoln said something to the effect that, God must love average and poor men, because He created so many of them. Whether it's average or poor, I have qualified on both counts. Most have. It is to those people, my comrades, who struggle daily with obscurity, drabness and wanting their lives to count for something that this book is dedicated.

If any one verse in the Bible speaks to the yearning in my heart to realize a meaningful destiny, it is Romans 8:28. I especially like the way British theologian and Biblical translator J.B. Phillips renders the passage: "Moreover we know that to those who love God, who are called according to His plan, everything that happens fits into a *pattern for good.*" [18]

It is my hope and prayer that this study of destiny will be stimulating and personally valuable as you wrestle with your destiny—a living history that can be significant, now and in eternity.

1
Looking Backward, Inward, and Upward

A Quest for Purpose: A Pilgrimage Begins • from Chapter One

This workbook will guide you through the text of *Wrestling with Destiny, A Layman Searches for Joy, Purpose and Fruitfulness*. The material is designed to help people understand their yearning for spiritual purpose, how it developed within them and how it can be cultivated in life.

The concept of destiny can be daunting. However, in the Bible the word is interpreted as appointment. God has appointments for us. Appointments lead us to our purpose. God's purposes for us are significant. Purpose realized leads to a destiny of significance.

1. Your past is literally a history of appointments that have been realized. They are comprised of people and events that deeply affected your values. This, in turn, is influencing the direction of your life. We encourage you to answer the following questions, meditate on your answers and discuss them with a trusted friend or small group.

Experiences that influenced me: *How it affected my perspective:*

_____   _____

_____   _____

_____   _____

_____   _____

_____   _____

2. All people, prominent and obscure, long for purpose. Worldly success does not guarantee a life of significance, but God desires that we experience lives of significance.

Complete this sentence: I would feel a deep sense of purpose and fulfillment if...

_____

_____

_____

_____

What have you done or what are you doing that you feel is a waste of your time and energy?

_____

_____

_____

_____

_____

How could you view your circumstances differently, realizing that God has ordained them and that He uses all things for good?

_____

_____

_____

_____

_____

CHAPTER TWO
Existing Foundations

1

Consider Your Foundation

I love the scene in *Planes, Trains & Automobiles* when Steve Martin and John Candy are driving the wrong way down an interstate. A couple yells to them "You're going the wrong way!" Candy then smugly asks: "How do they know where we're going?" And Martin concurs: "Yeah, how do they know?" Then, they look up and see two semi-trailers heading straight for them. They barely squeeze between the trucks and are sideswiped on both sides of their car. Sparks fly, and Candy, realizing he is facing death, has a vision of a ghoulish, laughing devil waiting for him.

We can be that way, honestly thinking we're heading in the right direction in our search for joy, purpose and fruitfulness. But in reality, unless we change direction, our efforts will be to no avail. That requires an assessment of the foundation we are building upon.

We once had a frightening experience that illustrates this truth. Kathy and I went on a camping trip in the remote and rugged Flat Tops Wilderness area. It's an isolated spot, deep in the White River National Forest of western Colorado. One day we went hiking and ended up far from camp. Then late in the day, as we were working our way back to camp, a weather system suddenly came rolling over the tops of the mountains. This can happen quite unexpectedly in the high country. Gone was the beautiful blue sky. It was quickly replaced by wind and rain. But I was confident that I knew my way back to camp, so confident that I wasn't using a compass—a foolhardy thing to do.

Then two bad things happened. First, the rain subsided into a slight drizzle accompanied by fog. Secondly, it got dark. I'd let too much time elapse before hiking back to camp.

There we were, cold and wet, aimlessly hiking around in a grey light that was rapidly turning black. But I had picked my landmarks, and I was sure we were heading the right way. However, between the fog and the poor light, the landmarks were disappearing.

Kathy became frightened, as she contemplated what could happen to us. It was October, the temperatures would be dropping rapidly, and we were wet. This is the perfect scenario for hypothermia, which can be deadly.

I, too, had these fears, and they were compounded by the guilt I felt for vainly and foolishly leading us into this predicament. We were totally lost, but my intuition told me that we were headed in the right direction. Several hours later, it was pitch black, as night had set in. Fortunately, we stumbled out of the forest onto a four-wheel drive road. Then, again thinking I was going the right way, I pointed us the wrong way down the road in the direction leading us further from the warmth and safety of our camp.

By God's grace, something happened that we thought was a miracle—a true deliverance. Lights appeared in the distance, and they were coming toward us. Soon we saw the two headlights of a small Jeep bouncing up and down over the rocks on the rugged road.

The driver was a nice person, and, better yet, he seemed to know the area well. We told him our dilemma and where we had made our camp. He graciously offered to take us there. I was quite surprised, however, when he turned the Jeep around and headed back down the road in the other direction. For the first time, I felt like we were headed the wrong way. But the driver seemed to think his way was right.

My navigating skills hadn't exactly impressed Kathy, so she asked me to just be quiet and ride. Then, after about an hour, there it was. What a blessed sight—our camp.

I remember being filled with a number of emotions, chief among them was relief. I also felt humiliated. I had foolishly put my wife's life at risk. I was full of thankfulness to the driver. He had driven several hours out of his way over difficult terrain, so we would be safe. He wouldn't let us do anything for him. We never even knew his name. Our "Good Samaritan" turned around and headed back up the road, out of our lives forever.

We make the same mistakes in our attempts to find joy, purpose and fruitfulness in life. We can honestly believe we are doing the right things and are following correct values, but that might not be so. We can have a faulty worldview.

A faulty worldview has implications. It leads to bad motives and poor decisions that can mark our lives with anxiety and stress. God uses these mistakes to show us that the natural inclinations of our own hearts are prone to error. If we're smart, we'll turn to Him for direction.

How do we acquire a faulty worldview? It can partially be attributed to baggage from the past, and we all have some. By baggage I mean core beliefs and values that we've developed that may not be true. Our baggage can leave us with a poor foundation to build upon. And bad beliefs have consequences.

By implication, our actions will be a reaction to our past, rather than proactive action based on the truth of God's Word. We have to be willing to honestly evaluate our core beliefs and values, testing them against God's truth. Our beliefs and values are either true, or they are baggage.

Here's a prominent source of baggage. I was talking to a person recently about the path her life had taken. We were talking about purpose, and she said: "Hey, I don't have a carefully thought out plan. But, I don't want to be like my parents. I don't want to go down that path, but I don't know how to get to any other." The more I thought about her comments the more I realized how often I'd heard this from people.

Even in the most loving families, negative things happen. Our sons are now adults with families of their own. We've had numerous conversations about how they were impacted by some of my decisions. I said and did things that left a lasting imprint on them. I began to feel that, as parents, we do the best we can for twenty-some years and then spend the rest of our lives asking for forgiveness from our children. I loved them greatly and tried hard to be a good parent. We are simply imperfect people.

It's like a human, emotional version of a drop forge in manufacturing. Early in my healthcare career, I worked in orthopedics, primarily with surgical implants, such as total hip and knee replacements. Consequently, I was often in the manufacturing plants where these ingenious devices were created. This was a remarkable process to observe. In fact, I would take groups of surgeons on tours of our factory for the promotional value. Molten metal would be placed beneath the drop forge, or press. Then the press would descend with great force, shaping the metal to make an implant.

That force is representative of the impact that people can have on each other, not only in the family, but in all relationships. Those things that frighten, hurt or anger us in our childhoods become baggage that we have to work through as adults. We are affected by the actions of others. We didn't have any power or control over many things that happened to us. We were, however, left to deal with the consequences. Such things can mark us for life.

That was true of my experience in the fast-food business as a boy. I realize that many people have had far worse childhood experiences. Nonetheless, I was angry because I had to work so much. It seemed to me that normal kids had paper routes or mowed lawns in the summers. They weren't working fourteen hours every day. I was miserable and came to believe work was evil. You had to do it for money. I was also frightened because money was something we didn't have enough of.

I did not grow up in a Christian home. I only recall going to church a few times as a boy, and then it was at the invitation of friends. Happily my parents both became Christians, but it occurred later in life. Hence, the truth of God's Word was not foundational to our family life. That left us with uncertainty and fear when it came to getting by financially. Consequently, I placed a lot of value on money and was determined to acquire as much as I could, so I'd never have to live like that again.

You can't have joy and purpose with those kinds of attitudes regarding work and money. My perceptions were far from God's revealed truths regarding these two important subjects. I had to change my worldview. That meant digging into the Bible and getting some good advice. Then, I had to believe what I'd learned was true, when my feelings were preconditioned to tell me otherwise.

Sometimes baggage can be hard to let go of because it can feel good. We get attached to the comfort it can create. For instance, as a result of my upbringing I believed buying things would make me happy. I really wanted to believe this, because I had gone without things for so long. Then later, when I started making money, I thought it was great fun to shop.

This was like a narcotic. After a while, "the thing" didn't satisfy, and I had to buy other things. Then I was exposed to God's teaching that ultimately things could not satisfy. It was sad to know this was true, although I'd always suspected it. In fact, I'd tried hard to disprove it. To change this habit was like losing an old friend who had comforted me during tough times. Like everyone I have some items that I enjoy, but now I try to shop only when I need to and don't see it as a recreational activity.

Fortunately, God is committed to changing our worldview. He interacts to lead us away from our baggage, our poor thinking. Again this reminds me of the forging process, and I only told you about the first half. After the implant is forged, it is x-rayed to see if there are flaws in its internal structure that could later break under stress. If a flaw is detected, the implant is reheated, turned again into molten metal and re-forged. This can happen over and over till there are no internal flaws. That's what God does with us.

Therefore, it's helpful to look *inward* to verify the trustworthiness of the assumptions that make up our worldview—interior re-forging so to speak. The circumstances of life will expose our flaws, and our worldview needs to be correct, if we are to fully experience joy, purpose and fruitfulness in life.

2
Survival, Success and Significance

I've noticed a pattern that is reflective of many life experiences. The pattern has helped me to identify flaws in my worldview. The pattern of life for many Americans has three distinct phases: as adults we move from *survival*, to *success*, to *significance*.

My starting point in adult life certainly was survival. When I think of survival, I think of my twenties—a decade I'd just as soon forget. I had finished school and my military commitment. I was launching into the world and was full of fear and insecurity. I wanted to prove to my family and my peers that I could succeed. But I was anxious because I wasn't sure that I could.

I was primarily concerned with survival. Luckily, I got a job, but it wasn't the one I wanted. It wasn't even in my field of choice. But I was married and had started a family. There were people to care for. There were many bills and limited income. It was an adult version of the same life I knew as a kid.

Then, because my core values weren't right, I created even more baggage. My false belief in the importance of things quickly led to credit card debt. It was a form of entrapment that stifled my attempts to live purposely. I was consumed with digging out of a financial hole.

I certainly wasn't thinking about anything profound like significance. I was too scared. The extent of my vision was a faint hope that I'd be able to care for my family. I felt trapped. I also fretted about losing my job. My original work had been in medical sales. I worried that I wouldn't hit my quotas, and I'd get fired. This fear coupled with a lack of vision and hope made for a drab existence.

I was also prone toward depression. My depression had nothing to do with a physiological problem. My skewed worldview created the depression. It was like driving in a rainstorm on the highway. I'd see a black cloud approaching, and all I could do was drive on until I finally drove through the storm. It was debilitating and would typically last for several weeks.

One of the things I most appreciate about God is that He continues to replace my faulty worldview with His truth. More often than not, His truth cures my depression. Now when I get depressed, I quickly realize it's probably because I have a wrong perception regarding something. By turning to the Bible, I can identify my problem thinking. Depression is avoided by seeing truth, believing it and then taking the appropriate action.

Many people move past the survival phase and experience success. They get promoted, make money, acquire material possessions, and develop a net worth. Society says such accomplishments are indicative of success. These are the people who are anxious to go to their class reunions. They've accomplished something they're proud of and want people to know it.

Often people become trapped there because success can be alluring and intoxicating. Others don't know how to move on. Some think that success is significance and never contemplate the third stage at all. One of my favorite writers, Os Guinness, said: "Success may then flatter us on the outside as significance eludes us from the inside." [19]

The pattern isn't true for everyone. There's another possibility. The survival stage may be one's lot in life. We don't aspire to that, but apparently it's a reality.

Jesus said: "For the poor you will always have with you." [20] Evidently, there will always be a lower, middle and upper class. However, the numbers seem to be skewed toward the lower classes. I've heard that in the U.S., less than two percent ever reach what might be called true financial independence.

How do we measure success anyway? Your idea of success probably isn't the same as mine. It might not even involve the idea of financial independence. Some of the most successful people I know don't have prestigious titles or lots of money. But those things are typically associated with the worldview of success.

The good news is that God has made provision for all this. In His genius and fairness, He has ensured that anyone can live a life of success and significance, regardless of their status in life. This is dependant upon believing the right things, having the right motives and reacting properly to life's situations with faith and obedience.

We must replace our misconceptions about success and significance and adopt God's viewpoint. In the next chapter, we'll discuss God's ideas regarding success and significance.

3
Three Lives

Let's look at three lives to help understand the difference between a faulty worldview and a solid foundation upon which we can build a life of significance. I'll discuss aspects from the lives of the Apostle Paul, the renowned missionary Oswald Chambers and my own.

Paul and Chambers are worthy of emulation. After proper evaluation, they changed their worldviews. Then they were able to properly respond to their appointments with faith and obedience.

Unfortunately, my example will provide a contrast to the right way. By studying these three examples, we can identify a mental perspective that has the ability to endure. We have a part to play, and that's to try to have a proper value system, or worldview, that leads us to proper actions.

We'll never affect how much God loves us. That will always be a full, complete love. But a faulty worldview can compromise our effectiveness for Him. Consider this statement the Apostle Paul made to his disciple, Timothy:

> In a wealthy home some utensils are made of gold and silver, and some are made of wood and clay. The expensive utensils are used for special occasions, and the cheap ones for everyday use. If you keep yourself pure, you will be a utensil God can use for His purpose. Your life will be clean, and you will be ready for the Master to use you for every good work. [21]

4
Two Fundamental Questions

I came to grips with the fact that I needed to forget about the world's view of survival and success. I needed to pursue the things that God viewed as significant. However, I felt somewhat paralyzed. What should I do with my life? Should I change jobs, move or go to seminary? The decisions I needed to make seemed endless.

Destiny seemed complex. But was it really? There were many questions. Was my destiny simply inevitable fate? Could it be grasped and shaped by willpower? What was the balance between God's involvement and my own? Theologians over the years have never fully explained any of these things. Thankfully, God gives us clues to illuminate the way.

I found one such clue in Anne Lamott's book, *Bird by Bird*. She gave a helpful illustration that can be applied to this problem: "Thirty years ago my older brother, who was ten years old at the time, was trying to get a report on birds written that he'd had three months to write. It was due the next day. We were out at our family cabin in Bolinas, and he was at the kitchen table close to tears, surrounded by binder paper and pencils and unopened books on birds, immobilized by the hugeness of the task ahead. Then my father sat down beside him, put his arm around my brother's shoulder, and said, 'Bird by bird, buddy. Just take it bird by bird.'" [22]

I wish I had heard that forty years ago. However, as I searched for direction, I found in the Bible an example that helped me unravel this complex question of what to do next.

When the Apostle Paul came to that strategic point in his life, he quickly reduced the complexity down to two questions, maybe the most important questions we'll ever ask in life:

1. *Who is the Lord?*
2. *What does He want me to do?*

My view of God determines everything I do. My actions follow my beliefs.

5

A Man on the "Fast Track" to Success

When Paul first posed those two profound questions, he was striving for success, endeavoring to become a prominent figure in Judaism. He had all the best credentials, having been born into the right tribe and family. He had received the finest education available to a Jewish youth. He had the right title, quickly rising to become a

Pharisee at an early age. I can just picture him—competitive, intense and driven. I imagine him at the time being self-righteous with a veneer of humility.

Paul had become a fanatical persecutor of Christians, believing he was offering service to God. As he was journeying to Damascus to persecute Christians, he had his fateful encounter with Jesus Christ. A bright light flashed from the heavens blinding Paul. He fell to the ground and instinctively uttered two critical questions: "Who are You, Lord?" and "What shall I do Lord?" [23]

He quickly summarized the central issues of life. It doesn't get more concise than that. Then, Jesus responded to Paul's questions with a statement alluding to his destiny—the role Paul was to play in history. "Get up and go on into Damascus, and there you will be told of all that has been *appointed* for you to do." [24]

He didn't give Paul more information than he needed, only the next step. That's a principle worth noting. It helps to untangle the complexity of what to do. Listen to Jesus, and He'll tell you the next step to take, one "bird" at a time. If that sounds overly simplistic, it is.

This reminds me of a statement by novelist E.L. Doctorow. He was referring to elements of writing, but his statement applies here as well. He said: "This is like driving a car at night. You can only see as far as your headlights, but you can make the whole trip that way." [25]

Therefore, the first step is to be obedient in the immediate situation, focusing on what you can see.

6

Self-Interest and Destiny

Paul had chosen to become a Pharisee. Ironically, our quest for joy, purpose and fruitfulness usually starts with self-interest. That's a good indicator of baggage. Ask yourself the following question: If I live by this core belief, who will it glorify, me or God? The answer can be quite revealing.

However, God honors man's free will. Consequently, often we are manipulative, trying to control our destinies, attempting to create the result that we envision for ourselves.

Paul's worldview was that joy, purpose and fruitfulness are realized through religious accomplishment, and he threw himself wholeheartedly into the task. His comments in Philippians 3:4-6 indicate that his faith and confidence weren't in God, but in his credentials and zeal—in reality, a religious competitive spirit. That's baggage, and it was leading him down the wrong path.

God leads us away from our visions for self-realization eventually. If we are to have lives of significance, we must be willing to let go of our visions for self-realization. Instead, we should focus on Paul's questions: "Who are You Lord," and "What do You want me to do?"

Walt Henrichsen has an interesting saying about how we move away from a faulty worldview. He says the change can occur in three successive stages:

Stage 1. *In the beginning, we do wrong things for wrong reasons.*

Stage 2. *Then, we do right things, but for wrong reasons.*

Stage 3. *God's goal, however, is that we do right things for the right reasons.*

Here's what those stages can look like, using the evolution of my attitudes toward dating and marriage as an example.

Stage 1. *Doing the wrong thing, for the wrong reason.*

As a teenager, my attitudes toward dating centered on my self-gratification. Sadly, I picked the wrong role model—James Bond. The Bond movie *From Russia with Love* came out in 1963, when I was in high school. All the guys thought he was very cool, and we all wanted to be like him. He was handsome, well dressed, got all the girls, drove neat cars, and lived an adventurous life. Being an avid reader, I read the entire Bond series by Ian Fleming.

Needless to say, this influence led to wrong actions fueled by wrong motives. I might have thought I was cool like James Bond. In reality, my faulty worldview regarding sexuality was destructive.

Stage 2. *Doing the right thing, for the wrong reason.*

Then, two significant but unrelated things happened. I met Kathy, and I became a Christian. I started doing right things but for the wrong reasons. We married after dating for six years. That was the right thing to do. But my view of marriage wasn't appropriate in the beginning. My focus was on her fulfilling my needs, rather than on me fulfilling hers. I was self-absorbed, and that's obviously not God's view of marriage.

Stage 3. *Doing the right thing, for the right reason.*

I finally started to understand that Christ wanted me to love my wife sacrificially, like He loves His Church. I realized that marriage wasn't about me being "the king of my castle."

As I came to understand God's view of marriage, I became more the husband He intended me to be. I started doing right things for right reasons. I tried to replace selfishness with selflessness. Needless to say, we're both a lot happier.

7
Do I Know What's Best for Me?

Paul's encounter with Jesus Christ and Walt's three stages beg the question: do we really know what's best for us? I've concluded that we don't—only God does. In reality, faulty worldviews are harmful, and self-interest can't be trusted.

Before Paul had his encounter with Christ, he absolutely believed he was doing the right thing with his life. But he wasn't. He was like me, aimlessly leading Kathy in the mountains, all the while thinking I knew where I was going.

Paul didn't understand his own heart. The Hebrew concept of heart involved four things: the reasoning process, the emotions, convictions and the will. Paul's heart had him headed in the wrong direction. God intervened, changed his heart and led him down a different path toward his true purpose in life. Paul had to submit to that, in spite of his intuition and trust that this new way was right.

I equate my common sense with my heart. As I reason through various issues and aspects of life, emotions are created. As a result, convictions are developed. Then I make decisions and take action. My common sense assures me that I've done the logical, wise thing. But often that's not true.

The beautiful promise exists that God will help us: "And your ears will hear a word behind you, 'This is the way, walk in it,' whenever you turn to the right or the left" [26]—just like our deliverer in the wilderness.

We have to accept by faith, just like Paul, that our new direction is right. As we abandon our old way, we find that striving and anxiety is replaced by peace. This frees us from the process of creating our purpose. Instead, we are free to respond to purpose—one that God leads us to.

8
Who's in Control?

Paul's response to his dramatic encounter with Christ reveals another concept that's significant: God's authority to determine our destinies. This authority is something we try to usurp.

We don't let go of our worldviews easily. After all, it took years to sculpt them. We trust them. They have gotten us where we are, even though that might not be a good place.

The hardest part is that, with our faulty worldview, we feel we are in control. And control isn't something one gives up easily. We think we have the authority to craft our destinies, but in reality we don't. When we refuse to yield to God's authority, we create problems for ourselves.

Remember Paul's first question, "Who are you Lord?" Looking at the account of his experience in Acts 9, we see that Paul instinctively referred to Jesus Christ as Lord.

Granted, his experience was dramatic. Nonetheless, when you call someone Lord, you are acknowledging His authority. Christ's answer also alluded to His authority. To paraphrase, He said, "I am God, now arise and go. This is My world and My plan for the redemption of man. By My grace, if you are obedient, this is the part you will play. Now get moving."

Paul's later writings demonstrate a man deeply in love with Jesus. But initially, he hadn't had the time to know Him intimately. His initial response was not based on love. It was an acknowledgement of authority. He responded out of principle, and maybe some fear, and fell in love later.

Paul responded in trust, faith, submission and obedience, quickly relinquishing his perceived right to determine his lot in life. Then we see an intertwining of supernatural and circumstantial events that created a life of significance.

By contrast, my early decisions regarding the direction of my life weren't the same. I had to learn who is in control the hard way. It was a sad and painful time of life. God used it for good, but I've always felt I inflicted needless suffering on Kathy and myself because of my manipulation and lack of willingness to trust God with my purpose. I forced God to drop the forge on me again.

Some are tempted to attribute every experience to God's will, and every experience certainly is that. However, God's Word also talks about a higher path that He makes available to us. When we don't choose to go down that path as a first alternative, He then takes us down another—the path of circumstantial suffering.

Paul speaks to this pathway when he admonishes the Corinthian Church for not partaking of communion appropriately. He said,

> But let a man examine himself, and so let him eat of the bread and drink of the cup. For he who eats and drinks, eats and drinks judgment to himself, if he does not judge the body rightly. For this reason many among you are sick and weak, and a number sleep. But if we judged ourselves rightly, we should not be judged. But when we are judged, we are disciplined by the Lord in order that we may not be condemned along with the world. [27]

I chose the latter path early in my career. I was anxious to run my own business in the field of orthopedics. But lucrative contracts with surgical implant manufacturers were scarce. I kept getting passed over when a contract became available. I was always told I was doing well but was too young.

I've already confessed to being competitive, intense and driven—I was an orthopedic version of Paul. I became manipulative and political, developing connections and cultivating relationships with all the leading companies. Some might say that's all part of doing business, that I was being smart, doing the right things. The problem was my efforts were born of self-will. I had no conviction or guidance that this was God's plan. I usurped His authority.

I came close to landing contracts several times only to have something happen at the last minute. One time, we even contracted for a home in another city, put together office space, formed banking relationships and sold our home in Colorado, only to have everything ultimately unravel. I just couldn't make it happen, and I was upset at God for not blessing my aspirations.

Then a real problem occurred. My employer told me to do something that was blatantly dishonest. His request came with a threat. If I didn't do it, I'd have to leave. He was already upset with me, because he knew I wanted to leave, and that would be disruptive to his business.

I only had one choice—resign, which I did on the spot. There went my income. I was hurt and perplexed. I hadn't done anything wrong. Actually, my refusal to do wrong cost me my job. That didn't seem fair.

Simultaneously my negotiations with several orthopaedic companies fell apart. All my efforts to control my destiny were futile. Although perplexed, my anger with God subsided quickly. It seemed incongruous to be mad and plead for help at the same time. I didn't understand the situation but was more concerned with survival. The unemployment lingered for months. We quickly used up our savings, and I was concerned about our financial doom.

Then, I got to witness the beauty of God's guidance, intervention and authority. By that point, I was beaten down by the process and had become very contrite. One night, I got a call from the orthopedic company about a contract that we'd almost finalized. Ironically, this was the same company that contracted with my ex-employer. Their representative asked me to meet him later that night at a remote park on the edge of the city.

That seemed odd. It was very "cloak and daggerish." It was like the scene in *All the President's Men*, when the key insider, referred to as "Deep Throat," shows up in his trench coat with information and guidance for Robert Redford and Dustin Hoffman.

When I arrived at the park, the representative was wearing a trench coat. He stood in front of his car, silhouetted by the headlights. I had to laugh. I asked him what was wrong with a hotel or a restaurant? He was adamant about not being seen. After he told me what had happened, I could understand why.

Evidently, my ex-employer had a propensity for doing dishonest things. He had been caught in what's considered white-collar criminal activity by several federal law enforcement agencies. It was about to cost him his business. The company contact was asking me to enter into a partnership and assume the contract.

This was a major opportunity, more significant than anything I had been negotiating. God had been watching the cheating and decided to judge those activities. In the process, He taught me lessons about not usurping His authority. His judgment confirmed that, this indeed was the direction my life was supposed to take. But it was going to happen His way and on His timetable.

My worldview changed that night in the park. God's intervention was so obvious in these events. I had done absolutely nothing, and everything I'd strived years for was given to me. God didn't need my efforts to make that happen.

Consequently, today, when adversity strikes, I am not as prone to action. I am more inclined to wait and see how things evolve. Part of my manipulative nature died that night.

There is great freedom in this, because we don't have to worry about creating our own destinies. We have to focus on our relationship with Jesus Christ and ask: "Who are you, Lord?" Then, over time, our appointments will be revealed to us.

We can make another interesting observation as we look at the circumstances of Paul's life. He certainly had a significant life. Yet, in a worldly sense, he lived in the *survival stage*. The man had nothing.

In fact, he purposely walked away from what the world would call success. Why? He said:

> I once thought all these things were so very important, but now I consider them worthless because of what Christ has done. Yes, everything is worthless when compared with the priceless gain of knowing Christ Jesus my Lord. I have discarded everything else, counting it all as garbage, so that I may have Christ and become one with Him. [28]

9
Relationship and Destiny

Paul had traded all of his worldly ambitions, his concept of his personal destiny, for something he deemed far more valuable—a *relationship*.

If I were to reduce the essence of the Bible to one word, I would choose the word relationship. It's about how man can relate to God, to other people and to the world around him. In the Bible, God is depicted as a personal God who loves people. As a result of this love, He is a pro-active God, intimately involved in the affairs of man. What was the under-girding truth behind Paul's two questions? It was relationship.

Paul wanted to be correctly related to God and to God's plan for his life. If we really believe that the relationship to Jesus is ultimately the most valuable thing in life, then we will abandon a faulty world-view and focus on that relationship.

Before making this decision, our lives are marked by striving and busyness. We're determined to get what the world tells us is valuable, such as money, status, possessions, and beauty. We frantically scurry about hoping our efforts will bring about the fulfillment of our dreams.

Jesus said: "If you try to keep your life for yourself, you will lose it. But if you give up your life for me, you will find true life." [29]

The renowned missionary and martyr Jim Elliott, commenting

on this truth, said: "He is no fool who gives what he cannot keep to gain what he cannot lose." [30]

Focusing on this issue of relationship, let's look at the life of Oswald Chambers. Like Paul, Chambers had a fruitful and significant life. It is said that his devotional book, *My Utmost for His Highest,* is the second most purchased book of all time, preceded only by the Bible. Chambers' influence has been vast and timeless.

However, his life also followed the three stages described by Walt Henrichsen. As a young man, he had a vision for his life apart from God. Then, he became a Christian and dedicated his life to God but asked God to bless his life on his own terms. Then, he truly gave his life to God and died to his own aspirations. Finally, he wanted only God and trusted God with his ultimate purpose.

As a young man, he wrote the following entry in his diary that referred to his sense of destiny: "From my very early childhood the persuasion has been that of a work, strange and great, an experience deep and peculiar, it has haunted me ever and ever." [31]

What he had desired was a career in the arts, an area that he dearly loved. After becoming a Christian, he dedicated his career to God. But art was still his career. He wanted to be God's man in the world of art.

Then he made a significant transition. David McCaslind, in his excellent biography, *Oswald Chambers—Abandoned to God,* wrote of the moment:

> Oswald had no idea what lay ahead as he boarded a train bound for Glasgow, then further west to Gourock, where he would catch a steamer across the Firth of Clyde. He knew only that his aim had once been art for God. Now it was only God. [32]

This transition allowed Chambers to experience the joy of discovering God's appointments for him. What was the significant transition Chambers made? He moved from wanting what God could do for him to purely wanting God.

It's ironic that often God gives people the desires of their hearts.

Again, Paul and Chambers are appropriate examples. Paul wanted desperately to be known as a great religious leader. He eventually did, only in a different religion and in a way that he could never have imagined. God granted his request. But God changed Paul in the process. By the time Paul became a great religious leader, he didn't see himself as one. He saw himself as something quite different. "...Jesus Christ came into the world to save sinners, among whom I am foremost of all." [33]

Chambers, likewise, became a great man of the arts. His writings have influenced countless numbers of people. Ironically, he never wrote anything. His writings actually are the dictated notes from his various speeches and teachings compiled by his wife years after his death.

When I read *My Utmost for His Highest*, I feel real power, but the power I sense is not Chambers the man. It is an encounter with Jesus Christ resident within the man. When I study the life of Oswald Chambers, I find a man focused on a relationship that led to a significant destiny.

10
Father Knows Best

We see in Paul and Chambers men who yielded their own aspirations for significance to the authority of Christ. They ceased striving and abandoned themselves to God. They focused on the relationship to Jesus Christ. Then, they responded with faith and obedience as God disclosed their appointments, one at a time. They were men building on the right foundations.

As they moved from survival to success to significance, these men, from a worldly perspective never progressed out of the survival stage. Yet they truly led lives of significance. They had nothing by the world's standards. They'd probably refer to that first stage as faith and dependence, not survival. In fact, they purposely chose to stay there, trusting God.

Martin Luther said: "I have held many things in my hands, and

I have lost them all. But whatever I have placed in God's hands, that I still possess." [34]

11

Faulty vs. True

What are the differences between Paul, Chambers and me? There are many:

A Faulty Worldview	True Worldview
• Usurped God's authority	• Recognized God's authority
• Focused on the calling	• Focused on the relationship
• Striving	• Abandonment
• Anxiety	• Peace
• Manipulation/control	• Let go
• Closed to other options	• Open to other options
• Defined next steps	• Responded in faith/obedience
• Anger	• Trust
• Thought I knew my own heart	• Yielded to God's insights
• Fought God's leading	• Submitted to God's leading
• Measured significance by what I did	• Measured significance by knowing Christ
• Glorified self	• Glorified God

Before you can build a house, you need a good foundation. That is also true in life, if we are to live in a way that will not compromise our joy, purpose and fruitfulness.

What forms your foundation? Do you have a vision for your life? Will it lead to the glorification of self or draw you closer to God? Would you describe your life as anxious and driven, or are you living one day at a time, responding in faith and obedience to the appointments He places before you?

When it comes to answering those two profound questions, how do you respond? Who is Jesus Christ? Do you believe in Him? If you do, is He perceived as a blessing machine in Heaven, whose job is to honor man's self-ordained aspirations? Do you want Jesus Christ or only what He can do for you? Do you believe He can be trusted?

Ask yourself these questions. Your answers might reveal baggage that you should let go of. It could be detrimental, robbing you of joy, purpose and fruitfulness.

WORKBOOK SECTION

1
Looking Backward, Inward, and Upward

Existing Foundations • from Chapter Two

We can honestly believe we are doing the right things according to correct values, but that might not be so. As illustrated in *Wrestling with Destiny*, we can have a faulty worldview. It can be partially attributed to baggage from the past that leaves us with a poor foundation upon which to build. Unfortunately, bad beliefs have consequences. Often our actions are predicated by our reaction to the past rather than proactive action based on God's Word.

3. Things that frighten, hurt or anger us in childhood become baggage we have to work through as adults.

What consequences have you had to deal with as a result of your childhood experiences?

_____

_____

_____

_____

_____

_____

_____

_____

4. A faulty worldview creates problem thinking. A simple exercise adapted from Lawrence Crabb's book, *Effective Biblical Counseling*, can help in our quest to identify problem thinking. As seen from the illustration below, an event occurs, and we have a choice to evaluate the event properly. We can determine whether we are wise or foolish by the emotion that arises from our choice.

For example, we once hired a rental company to provide tables, chairs and tablecloths for a banquet for our son's soccer team. However, the rental company never showed up. I called and yelled at the people responsible because they had ruined the evening. The event itself did not cause the emotion of anger. My evaluation of the event caused the emotion of anger. Any time I experience negative emotions, I can always go back to a moment when I evaluated an event improperly. At the point of evaluation, I can choose to change my faulty thinking with a Biblical truth.

Event

Rental company does not show up with tables, etc., for soccer banquet.

Evaluation

I am personally humiliated because this was my responsibility.
I blame them and yell at them because of their negligence.

Emotion

ANGER

Draw your own example in the space provided below. How did your evaluation of an event precipitate your emotions?

How could you have responded differently that would have reflected the fruit of the Spirit from Galatians 5:22-23: love, joy, peace, patience, kindness, goodness, faithfulness, gentleness, self-control?

_____

_____

_____

_____

5. St. Paul was a man appointed by God. In Acts, Paul was confronted with two fundamental questions relative to everyone's destiny: "Who art thou, Lord?" (Acts 22:8) and "What shall I do, Lord?" (Acts 22:10)

Briefly answer these two fundamental questions: How do you view the Lord? At this time, what do you think He is telling you to do?

_____

_____

_____

_____

6. A good indicator of whether or not we are motivated by self-interest is to ask ourselves the question: "Who will it glorify, me or God?" List your core beliefs. Put a checkmark by all those beliefs that glorify yourself rather than God.

○ _____

○ _____

○ _____

○ _____

7. As was discussed in the book, we can move away from a faulty worldview in three stages: doing the wrong things for the wrong reasons, doing the right things for the wrong reasons, doing the right things for the right reasons. Give an example from your past of each of these stages.

Stage 1: *Wrong things for wrong reasons:*

_____

_____

Stage 2: *Right things for wrong reasons:*

_____

_____

Stage 3: *Right things for right reasons:*

_____

_____

8. Contrast what you now believe to be a faulty worldview, based on more recently learned Biblical truth.

Faulty worldview: *Biblical truth:*

_____   _____

_____   _____

_____   _____

_____   _____

_____   _____

_____   _____

CHAPTER THREE
Proper Foundations

1
Searching for What's Really True

It was early Christmas Eve morning. I was anxious to get downstairs to our family room and enjoy the ambiance of a glowing fire in the fireplace. I poured a cup of coffee and settled into my favorite chair. Then I opened a golf magazine that had just come in the mail and proceeded to browse through its contents.

On the cover was an alluring picture of a golf course in the California Desert. I love the desert, and it was a cold, snowbound morning in Colorado. I felt covetous. It would sure be nice to be there playing golf.

Then page one had a picture of a sleek sports car speeding around a curve with a picturesque view of the ocean in the background. Now I was coveting the sports car. On the next page was an attractive couple sitting on a beach in the Caribbean. They smiled contentedly as they were being served exotic drinks. They seemed to be having a wonderful time. That looked enticing, as I pictured Kathy and myself in their place.

Soon I felt frustrated and discontented. Are all of those things true of life, I wondered? I reviewed the pages again but thought of other aspects of what I'd seen.

Yes, the mountains were cold and snowy, but at the same time, I was cozy by the fire. Plus, we love to ski, and you can't do that in the desert. We once lived in the California desert and didn't think 118 degrees in the summer was much fun.

I also owned a sports car once, just like the one pictured. I remembered how it broke down, leaving me stranded on lonesome roads on two occasions. Those events were followed by expensive, frustrating experiences with an auto dealership trying to get my car fixed.

How about the exotic island experience? We had been to Hawaii just the month before, and I recalled a number of things. First, there was the stress of going through airport security, and then there was the confrontation with the rental car company, which felt like a tropical version of Steve Martin's car rental scene from *Planes, Trains & Automobiles.*

I recalled the family with the rowdy and noisy children that occupied the room next to ours at the resort. The parents apologized every morning, saying they hoped their kids hadn't disturbed us. But they had!

One evening we were enjoying a terrific setting and a romantic dinner. It was a balmy night with a calm ocean breeze blowing. The beach was some fifty yards from our table. The waves were gently rolling to shore. Light glowed from the torches burning near by. However, the tranquility and romance were constantly interrupted by ringing cell phones. It made the evening memorable but for the wrong reason.

There are two sides to every story, I mused. I chuckled at myself and put the magazine down, concluding that I was looking for happiness in the wrong place. I reached for my Bible instead.

2
Let's Get Our Definitions Straight

Turning the focus *upward* to discuss God's values, let's address a word pertinent to the conversation: happiness. This can be both a frustrating word and a great word. I just wish I could have more of it. However, the word has an illusive quality.

In my quest for happiness, I've often responded to the advertisements similar to the ones I read on Christmas Eve morning. I get frustrated with myself when I do. Again, it's part of accepting a faulty worldview.

According to advertising, we can find happiness if we experience a certain thing, or look a special way, or own the right stuff, or feel an intense emotion, or have a particular vocation, or live in an exotic area, or have a relationship with that special person, or be like somebody else, etc.

If happiness is such an important word, and it's so necessary for our fulfillment, then how come Jesus never used it or promised it to us? He did say: "I came so that they might have life and have it abundantly." [35] Why didn't He use the word happiness? You'd think happiness would be central to abundant living.

Webster's dictionary defines happiness as being characterized by luck, good fortune and prosperity. Who in their right mind doesn't want such things? So, there must be a difference between the happiness of the world and the abundant life Jesus promised.

To further complicate things, Jesus tells us: "In the world you have tribulation," [36] a word defined as affliction or anguish. Although I don't look for it, tribulation seems to be easier to find than happiness.

Then Jesus makes a radical claim, that we can experience peace in the midst of tribulation. "These things I have spoken to you, that in me you may have peace. In the world you will have tribulation; but be of good cheer, I have overcome the world." [37] He even goes so far as to tell us to be cheerful about this.

Let's look at His promise of peace first. That's something we all want. A few chapters earlier in John, Jesus says: "I am leaving you with a gift—peace of mind and heart. And the peace I give isn't like the peace the world gives. So don't be troubled or afraid." [38]

He acknowledges that there is a worldview of peace but implies that His view is different and superior. Therefore, we can be cheerful even in tribulation.

The peace of Jesus is akin to hope. Author and journalist G.K. Chesterton said: "Hope is the power of being cheerful in circumstances that we know to be desperate." [39]

Sometimes desperate circumstances for me have involved litigation. It's hard to be in business today and avoid it. Lawsuits are typically confrontational and accusatory with the risk of personal loss. You can lose many things—reputation, relationships, opportunities and personal assets. Certainly, litigation is among one of the more unpleasant things in life.

To this day, when I get a certified letter that I'm not expecting, my initial reaction is anxiety. Someone is after me. This reminds me of how I felt as a kid when I knew I had done something wrong. It was just a matter of time until dad got home from work and disciplined me. Part of the anxiety was waiting for him to arrive. Those days were long.

However, I've always come away from litigations encouraged. Such times reveal the steady character and dependability of God. His Word put things in perspective, neutralizing the pain of the incidents and reminding me that the suits wouldn't mean anything in eternity. His promises of provision were comforting.

Dallas Willard, in *Renovation of the Heart,* defines Biblical peace in the following way: "Peace is the rest of will that results from assurance about 'how things will turn out.' 'I am at peace about it,' we say, and this means I am no longer striving inwardly or outwardly, to save some outcome dear to me or to avoid one that I reject." [40]

Now I can see a difference between the peace of Jesus and the worldview of peace. In the world, peace comes with conditions. Things have to turn out a certain way, or they will not create happiness. Tribulation is obviously not one of those conditions. But with Jesus we can have peace amidst tribulation.

Then He makes another seemingly outrageous claim: "But now I come to you; and these things I speak in the world, that they may have my joy made full in themselves." [41]

Here He promises us joy, a full and complete type of joy. Again, Dallas Willard describes this joy in the following way: "Joy is a pervasive sense—not just a thought—of well-being: of overall and ultimate well-being." [42]

Joy is a word that Jesus used over and over again, as something He desired for us. Joy is a more profound word than happiness.

I recently had an experience that captured the difference between joy and happiness. I was having a lovely weekend with my wife. It was Saturday evening, and we were cooking dinner together, one of our favorite pastimes. Then I began to feel poorly, and the pain intensified during the weekend. But, being a typically vain and macho guy, I wouldn't listen to my wife's pleas to go to the hospital. Finally, it became too painful, so I relented. The result was an emergency surgery late Sunday evening.

Although this was not a happy experience, it was nonetheless joyous. As I lay in the hospital bed Monday, my mind was filled with thoughts of how blessed I was. Sure, I was in pain, but I felt better than I did before the surgery. Plus, I'd received great care. The doctors and nurses were gracious, professional and very conscientious, even though they had to come in at midnight to care for me.

Having had a long career in healthcare, I appreciated this. I felt thankful for the privilege of working in healthcare, especially now that I had been a recipient of its service.

I also appreciated my family and friends. Their love was demonstrated. I was surrounded by kindness. I was convicted that I needed to be a more sensitive, caring individual, like the people who supported me. Many people aren't surrounded by that kind of concern. This experience gave me a sense of God's provision and love. Life felt very sweet as I lay in the hospital contemplating the experience.

This had turned out okay, and my spirit sensed that this probably wouldn't be my last time in a hospital. My fear of dying diminished a little that day. In other words, I had a pervasive sense of well-being in spite of adverse circumstances. Things were well with my soul. I cherish that experience. God used it to teach me about life, and I consider myself blessed as a result.

However, happiness is fickle. It will only grace your life with its presence when you have luck, good fortune and prosperity. According to Jesus, life won't always be full of such things. But I can have a pervasive sense of well-being or joy in the good times and the bad. I can do this because I know that with Jesus, things will ultimately turn out well. Therefore, I experience peace. I don't need to strive and fret. This seems far superior.

Thank goodness for Jesus' honesty. He's never lied to me about the nature of life. However, the worldview of happiness is full of lies. Real love is nothing like what's depicted in our culture. Neither is true beauty. Are some of the world's heroes really worthy of emulation?

Finding true joy, purpose and fruitfulness comes from the pursuit of knowing God and embracing His values, not the world's. Let's look upward and study those values. Then, we can redirect and focus our lives on those things that can actually create spiritual happiness now and have the promise of reward in the future.

3
Two Significant Words

The Bible tells us that God's essential nature is love, (I John 4:16). Jesus showed that essential nature to the world. He was a man of character—divine character. That character manifested itself in numerous ways. He performed constant acts of love, kindness, forgiveness, faithfulness, empathy and on and on. Jesus' life impacted those with whom He came into contact. Character influences characters.

Those two words, character and characters, are what God says have transcendent value. They form the substance of what He promises to reward in eternity. Character means those qualities that are distinctive to an individual and differentiate that person from others. By characters, I simply mean people.

Looking to the word character, notice Jesus' admonitions to the seven churches of Asia Minor recorded in The Book of Revelation, chapters 2-4. Each admonition has four basic components.

1 First, He specifies a character trait to be abandoned or embraced.

2 Second, He follows with a challenge to action, "he who overcomes," [43] or changes their character.

3 Third, He states a promise of reward in eternity for that change in character.

4 Lastly, He issues a second challenge. "He, who has an ear, let him hear what the Spirit says to the churches." [44]

The New Living Translation uses the following treatment of this statement: "Anyone who is willing to hear should listen to the Spirit, and understand what the Spirit is saying to the churches."

A paraphrase might sound something like this: "Is anyone listening? This is a decision you need to make and then apply to your life." This is only one of many examples in the Bible that reinforce God's strong emphasis on character growth.

Another is seen in the Beatitudes listed in Matthew 5:2-11. These are all attributes, distinctions or character traits of His followers. He goes on to say that those who strive to manifest these traits will receive great reward in Heaven.

Even something as simple as giving someone a cup of water can be rewarded. Before He sent out His disciples, He said: "And if you give even a cup of cold water to one of the least of My followers, you will surely be rewarded." [45]

Giving someone a cup of cold water can be revealing. It reveals character. First, a person manifests spiritual sensitivity by recognizing the need. This implies an external focus rather than an inward, selfish focus. It leads to an interruption of plans, pausing to go fulfill the need of another, which is a very one-sided transaction. There's nothing in it for the giver. It is an act of spiritual sensitivity, generosity and hospitality—a demonstration of character.

Bruce Milne elaborated on the nature of character and reward when he wrote:

> Every kingdom work, whether publicly performed or privately endeavored, partakes of the kingdom's imperishable character. Every honest intention, every stumbling word of witness, every resistance of temptation, every motion of repentance, every gesture of concern, every routine engagement, every motion of worship, every struggle towards obedience, every mumbled prayer, everything, literally, which flows out of our faith—relationship with the Ever-Living One, will find its place in the ever-living heavenly order which will dawn at his coming. [46]

4
Rewards

Jesus' life was marked by marvelous character traits, and we are exhorted to be like Him. It's not that we seek the reward itself. We seek to please the Lord. "So our aim is to please Him always, whether we are here in this body or away from this body." [47]

God has promised to reward this pursuit of pleasing the Lord and striving to take on His character traits.

> Behold, I am coming quickly, and my reward is with Me, to render to every man according to what he has done. I am the Alpha and the Omega, the first and the last, the beginning and the end. Blessed are those who wash their robes, [i.e. grow in character], that they may have the right to the tree of life, and may enter by the gates into the city. [48]

This is an overwhelming offer. God doesn't have to do this. He chooses to. This is graciousness beyond comparison.

There's a proper fear of God and an improper fear of God. I used to read verses like the one just quoted and they scared me, but in the wrong way. I thought God might be like an ogre in the heavens, out to get me when I slip up. I would look at that verse and see only the part that said: "render to every man according to what he has done." There were many things I'd done that I wasn't interested in having rendered back to me.

I wouldn't take into consideration the "blessed are those who wash their robes" part of the passage. This implies taking action, ending negative behavior, replacing it with positive behavior and then being rewarded for it. It's as if God were saying: "Hey look, this isn't good for you. I'm not like that, and you shouldn't be either. So let's work on this. You'll be a lot happier now, and I'll reward you later for your efforts, because I love you and want what's best for you."

The only way I've been able to comprehend the idea of God rewarding me as I attempt to grow in character, is to reflect on my love for our boys.

It hurts when I observe them saying, doing or being something that I know will compromise their well-being. However, when I see change and witness good decisions turn into positive actions, I rejoice. There's nothing I won't do to encourage or support them. I like rewarding them for their efforts.

Within a loving parent's heart is a basic desire to bless and affirm their children. It's not much of a leap to see that this might be true of a loving, heavenly Father.

I once experienced this truth in a painful, yet beautiful way. It involved an incident with our younger son, Matt, when he was in high school. He was never rebellious, but he did go through a difficult period during his adolescent years. He was struggling with his self-image, exhibiting self-destructive behavior at times, and hanging out with kids who were a bad influence. We lived under this cloud for roughly four years, from seventh grade through his sophomore year in high school. We did our best to love him unconditionally, to be supportive and available, but it broke our hearts as we watched him struggle. We often worried for his very life.

Then one day, Kathy felt compelled to have a heart-to-heart chat with Matt. She told him that his approach to life didn't seem to be working and asked him if he was really happy. She challenged him to consider if he wanted to live that way the rest of his life or did he think it was time to try a different way. For some reason, this resonated with his spirit.

This was a defining moment in Matt's young life. He decided to change—to really change.

He exhibited his newfound conviction in a way that caused me to weep uncontrollably. I had just gotten home from a business trip and was sitting on our front porch, unwinding from my trip. Kathy came outside and said that Matt had a surprise for me. Inwardly I thought: Oh great, this will probably be a tattoo that I'm supposed to think is awesome. Instead, a different Matthew appeared. Gone were the old, ratty clothes and the greasy, shoulder-length hair. He was nicely dressed and well groomed. I almost didn't recognize him.

My mind was filled with the pain and worry of the previous years. It had really hurt, as we tried to love him amidst his ordeals and bad decision-making. Anyone who's ever parented a teenager knows exactly what I'm saying. We had a good, long cry together and listened to Matt tell us about his new approach to life. This was one of the emotional highlights of my life. I was happy for him. I was happy for us. And my heart relished having the opportunity to support, encourage and reward him.

It seems that might be the way God feels about His children. What do you think? Is He an ogre? Or is He a loving Heavenly Father?

5
Performance and Rewards

I used to think that God's primary objective for me was service, being involved in lots of spiritual activities. My performance was the way to store up rewards in heaven. That created pressure to perform, and it was stressful.

Yet as a parent I'm more concerned about what kind of men our sons are becoming, not what they are doing. Being precedes doing. When the boys focus on being the right kind of men, then everything they do reflects a higher quality.

That illustration has spiritual implications. It means that every moment of every day is an opportunity to grow in character, regardless of the activity. We need to recognize the relevance of the moment, think of pleasing God and react appropriately. Then our days are filled with purpose. We are storing up treasure in Heaven, as Jesus instructed in Matthew 6:20. God rewards us for who we are becoming.

Or we can have a complete lack of awareness of the opportunity before us. Then we go through the day frustrated. What was really a God-ordained appointment was seen only as an intrusion, not an opportunity to grow in character. This response squanders life.

That's also when we look for activities that we think are relevant, so we can perform and win the approval of God and man.

6
Character Influences People

Now, let's turn our attention to the word "characters." There is a place for service. It's just not intended to precede our focus on our relationship to Christ and our character growth. It's intended to flow from it.

Being does precede doing, but doing needs to occur. God also promises to reward us as we try to serve people in our spheres of influence—our families, neighbors and peers at work. We do that by exhibiting positive, selfless deeds and words of love that come from His Spirit working within us. This is a natural by-product of character growth. God does something in us, and it spills over into the lives of others, but our focus is on pleasing Him. There is something natural and authentic about our service when we focus primarily on pleasing Christ.

I have a friend who I've worked with over the years. Our relationship started in a natural way. His cubicle used to be outside my office. Consequently, he had opportunities to watch my responses to many situations. Fortunately, this was at a time when I was in a good place spiritually.

One day he walked into my office and paid me a compliment. He said he'd noticed that I reacted differently to circumstances than other executives he had worked for. What was up with that? I offered to take him to lunch and talk about it.

What followed were years of conversations about putting faith into practice in the business world. In other words, living in the moment, focusing on Jesus and letting Him use every experience to form His character within me. I love this man, and he loves me. Today we're still friends, and he's in business practicing the principles we have discussed.

I never had a compulsion to have a ministry in his life. In fact, I wasn't conscious of the affect I was having on him at all. I had a compulsion to respond to my appointments daily to please the Lord. The focus was on what God was doing in my life, and that ended up affecting a peer.

However, there is an opposite truth we should note regarding our service. We can mistakenly think God's interested primarily in our productivity, bringing people to a relationship with Christ and discipling them. The more we have in our trophy case the larger our reward will be.

I remember once, Kathy and I had several people over for dinner. All present were Christians except one lone soul. There was a conscious awareness of this among the rest as we sat around the dinner table. There was an unspoken compulsion to evangelize this person, lest we be judged by each other. This was a perverted form of spiritual competition—I'm godlier than you, and I'm going to prove it by sharing my faith with this cornered victim. We verbally pounced on this unfortunate person, each trying to control and guide the conversation. We had an agenda. We were on a mission.

Once I was on an outing in the mountains and saw a mountain lion attack a deer. It was fast, unseen and lethal. That's the way this was. The Spirit of God wasn't within a hundred miles of that dinner table. It was like reverse polarity with a magnet, as our words drove that person further away from Christ.

Granted, we had shared our faith, but we needed to be forgiven, not rewarded. It's amazing that we maintained the friendship. At the end of the evening, the individual took Kathy and me aside and begged us never to allow that to happen again. Our evangelism was a forced, unnatural act.

The Apostle Paul talked about natural love and service for Christ when he wrote to the Thessalonians: "We were gentle among you as a mother feeding and caring for her own children. We loved you so much that we gave you not only God's Good News but our own lives, too." [49] I can't think of anything in life that's purer and more natural than a mother's love.

In another epistle, Paul further illuminates this thought. The Corinthian believers had made a mistake in comparing Paul's work to that of another missionary—Apollos. In his response, we see more instruction regarding rewards for our efforts to influence others.

Who is Apollos, and who is Paul, that we should be the cause of such quarrels? Why, we're only servants. Through us God caused you to believe. Each of us did the work the Lord gave us. My job was to plant the seed in your hearts, and Apollos watered it, but it was God, not we, who made it grow. The one who plants and the one who waters work as a team with the same purpose. Yet they will be rewarded individually, according to their own hard work. We work together as partners who belong to God. You are God's field, God's building—not ours. [50]

The fruit, whatever it may be, comes from God and not us. Our job is obedience, trying to please Him with our lives, doing the best we can with what we have—one appointment at a time. That's what will be rewarded.

To illustrate this point, I'll be like Paul Harvey and "tell you the rest of the story" about Matt. After he decided to change, he never looked back. He went on to graduate from college with a degree in theatre and headed to L.A. to pursue his dreams of working in film.

He also fell in love with Jesus and longed to have a positive influence in the film media. In addition to Jesus, he fell in love with someone else. Miraculously among twelve million people, he met Regan, and she became his wife. She shares his convictions and is ideally suited for him. They're quite a team.

Everyone has opinions of Los Angeles. Steve Martin even made a movie, *L.A. Story,* satirizing his hometown. We personally like the area, but, as parents, we were concerned for his well-being when he told us what he wanted to do. We imagined our boy adrift in a sea of millions of people, all the while trying to break into a difficult industry. I wanted God to give me power of attorney in Matt's life, so I could tell him to do something else.

Fast-forwarding a few years, I can tell you that I was completely wrong. Matt and Regan have many friends and a fine church. And, after much hard work, Matt landed a job with a film production company.

Today they are influencing people. In my omniscience, I thought God had given up on Hollywood. Recently, three people individually came up to Matt and said that they had noticed that he approached his work differently. They thought it was because of his faith. They went on to say that they had spiritual issues they were trying to sort out. Would he talk with them about it or take them to church sometime?

My attitude had been similar to Elijah the prophet's recorded in I Kings 19. He was particularly displeased with the people of Israel and was complaining to God. The Lord reminded him that he had failed to notice at least 7,000 people who had never "bowed the knee to Baal or kissed him." [51] His plan was to save them.

Once, we were visiting Matt and Regan when they were hosting a big dinner party in their small, newlywed's apartment. When we walked in the front door, the first thing we noticed was the beautifully scripted menu for the evening that Regan had carefully written in crayon on the sliding glass door to their deck.

Then, they spent the night spoiling twenty-five or so of their friends with their good cooking. This was followed by an after dinner speaker addressing spiritual issues pertinent to young people today. We were all crammed into a room about the size of a large walk in closet, but everyone had a great time. This was not a one-time event. They do this often.

I'm delighted, but I'm a little ashamed of myself. This would not have been my plan for our son. Plus, as I alluded to, God evidently doesn't share my bias about Hollywood. I feel guilty about this every time we go to visit. On each trip, we meet more people we like and see more evidence of legitimate influence.

This is not just the babbling of a proud parent, although I am one. Matt and Regan's lives illustrate the point I am making. They took personal accountability for their growth in character and began to try to please Jesus. As they did this, they began to know Christ better. Then there was a natural influence that came from their lives that touched people in their spheres of influence.

It reminds me of the following verse:

Now wherever we go He uses us to tell others about the Lord and to spread the good news like a sweet perfume. Our lives are a fragrance presented by Christ to God. But this fragrance is perceived differently by those being saved and by those perishing. To those perishing, we are the fearful smell of death and gloom. But to those being saved we are a life giving perfume. [52]

What is the result? The kids have their share of problems and tribulation, but, by and large, they are experiencing a blessed life. And God will reward their efforts one day in eternity.

I need to follow their example. It's as if they are the parent, and I am the child. Our living room is bigger than a walk-in closet. However, I don't think we've ever had twenty-five people there at once.

To over-simplify the point, God's values center around His family. He's developing character in His children. Then He uses their character to adopt other children, adding characters to His family. Anything that we do to contribute to those efforts will be rewarded, now and in eternity.

In his book, *Heaven,* Randy Alcorn wrote: "Prior to Christ's return, his Kingdom will be intermingled with the world's cultures (Matthew 13:24-30). But his followers will be growing in character and proving their readiness to rule. Through adversity and opportunity, as well as in their artistic and cultural accomplishments, they will be groomed for their leadership roles in Christ's eternal Kingdom. Their society—transforming creative skills will be put on prominent display in the new universe, where they will 'shine like the sun in the Kingdom of their Father' (Matthew 13:43)." [53]

He goes on to say: "God is grooming us for leadership. He's watching to see how we demonstrate our faithfulness. He does that through his apprenticeship program, one that prepares us for Heaven. Christ is not simply preparing a place for us; he is preparing us for that place." [54]

7
The Clock Illustration

Visual illustrations have always helped me grasp tough concepts. Needless to say, understanding how God was working in my life in light of eternity was not an easy concept to grasp. Then, one day I stumbled onto something that really helped me see how God was using circumstances to affect my life daily. This visualization showed me how the experiences in my world were being used to affect my character and also influence characters. I hope it helps you.

Picture a clock in your mind's eye. Everything that happens to us occurs in time, and we are instructed to make the best use of it. Paul said: "Therefore be careful how you walk, not as unwise men, but as wise making the most of your time, because the days are evil." [55]

On this imaginary clock place the name of God at 12:00. Then, put your name at 6:00. Now, at 3:00 and again at 9:00 place the name of whatever it is that best describes your sphere of influence. You could name what you do, such as teacher, business owner or home-maker—whatever it is that is the essence of your world. It looks like this for me:

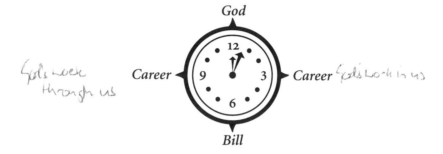

As I move through time toward 6:00, God uses my circumstances to cause me to grow in character. Then, as time goes on, moving from 6:00 back to 12:00, I can be used to impact people in my sphere of influence.

What I really appreciate about this is God's total utilization of every moment in my life. Every experience provides me with an opportunity to grow personally, to be fruitful and, according to His promise, to have a chance to store up reward in Heaven. Then, I am living by His values—moment by moment. When I really grasp this truth, my life is filled with an amazing amount of purpose.

I never thought I would say such a thing, but work is actually more fun than play because it's filled with spiritual purpose.

However, there's a requirement on my part. I must be alert spiritually. I must be sensitive to His Presence in my life moment by moment, or I'll miss what He's trying to do in me and through me.

I must confess, for many years I did not recognize this utilitarian aspect of God's character. Consequently, opportunities went unrecognized. But, virtually every instance is an opportunity for growth.

Take something as simple as driving a car. Are the things that happen to us behind the wheel just nuisances, or is there something of eternal value there? It depends on whether we have God's perspective or our own.

I recall a time when I was traveling with a business colleague. I was a mentor to this person spiritually. I was driving aggressively because we were running late for an appointment. In my mind, the slow traffic was an inconvenience. There was nothing spiritually redemptive about it. However, as I soon found out, my driving irritated my friend. I know this because he told me so, in no uncertain terms. As a result, my credibility dropped with him a little that day.

From God's perspective, this was an opportunity to consider my colleague's needs ahead of my own—always a good habit and reflective of Jesus' nature. Paul said: "Do not merely look out for your own personal interest, but also for the interest of others. Have this attitude in yourselves which is also in Christ Jesus." [56] This went totally unrecognized by me. I missed the significance of the appointment.

Jesus described the spirit behind the clock illustration when He said:

...The foremost [commandment] is, 'Hear O Israel; the Lord our God is one Lord; and you shall love the Lord your God with all your heart, and with all your soul, and with all your mind, and with all your strength.' The second is this, 'you shall love your neighbor as yourself.' There are no other commandments greater than these. [57]

Notice several points about His remarks. First He talked about our vertical relationship to God. Then He mentioned our horizontal relationships with people. My experience has been that it's important for me to focus on the first commandment before I can effectively carry out the second. It's easy to reverse the two and focus on people more than God, thereby compromising both relationships.

And how do we know if we are doing these two things—loving God and our neighbors? Jesus answers these questions. "He who has my commandments and keeps them, he it is who loves Me, and he who loves Me will be loved by My Father, and I will love him, and will disclose Myself to him." [58]

Keeping His commandments means obedience, focusing on pleasing Him, not on our service or spiritual production. If we do that first, we will naturally go on to love our neighbor the right way, having a positive influence on others.

Also note that as we seek to live by these values, He promises to disclose Himself to us. That word means to reveal, declare or to make known. Shedding more light on this, He said: "And this is the way to have eternal life—to know You, the only true God, and Jesus Christ, the one You sent to earth." [59]

When I think about Biblical figures that manifested a deep relationship with God, I often think of King David. What differentiated him from others? One characteristic stands out to me. He saw God in all things at all times. He had spiritual sensitivity. He said, "I know the Lord is always with me. I will not be shaken, because He is right beside me." [60]

This verse doesn't say that he only saw God in important matters. He never demonstrated the spiritual indifference that can victimize us, like I demonstrated with my driving story. David worked everything out in life prayerfully with God. He saw God in everything and dealt with circumstances and people with a spiritual perspective.

Although I try not to use colloquialisms, there's one I can't help using. It's easy to be "asleep at the switch." God's there, ready to disclose Himself to us in our circumstances. We're just not paying attention.

Do I ever think that some obnoxious person at the office can be used for spiritual good in my life? Am I busy trying to change jobs because it's uncomfortable? There are spiritual implications to all things.

As lay people, we can be tempted to believe that the only spiritually relevant parts of our lives happen at church or in Bible study groups. Sadly, I've known business people who hated their jobs and couldn't wait to retire and go do something "worthwhile" for the Lord, as if nothing spiritually significant happened during a thirty-year career. Do we really believe God is that wasteful? Remember, King David was a layman!

8

Comparing the Downstroke to the Upstroke

By way of a summary overview, let's compare moving through time from 12:00 to 6:00 and then moving back up toward 12:00, capturing the essence of what God is accomplishing through our lives.

As we move through time, He is using experiences and people in our sphere of influence at 3:00 to enhance our character. We are the primary focus, not others. At this stage, He is attempting to do a work in us. He is getting us to focus primarily on Him, so our responses to life come from His Spirit. As we move back toward 12:00, he is using us in our spheres of influence at 9:00 to influence others.

So we move from growth in character to influencing characters. First, He does a work in us, then through us. This allows us to utilize our vertical relationship with Him to relate horizontally to others. It looks like this:

12:00-6:00	*6:00-12:00*
Growth in character	Influencing characters
A work in me	A work through me
Internal process	External process
Focus on my world	Focus on the world of others
Vertical relationship first	Horizontal relationships second
God first	People second
Being	Doing
Relating to God	Reflecting that relationship to others

9
Where We've Been and Where We're Going

To reiterate, one of the purposes of this book is to discuss how we can more effectively experience joy, purpose and fruitfulness as lay people. We want to understand our appointments in life, respond to them obediently, and have a destiny marked by significance.

The first chapter talked about the importance of looking backward to identify those things that created the desire for a meaningful life.

The second chapter looked inward to challenge our core beliefs, to test whether or not they stand up to the scrutiny of scriptural truth. Significant lives cannot be built on the shaky foundation of core beliefs, motives and values that are not true.

The third chapter puts forth the proposition that joy, purpose and fruitfulness are best found in the pursuit of God's values. Looking upward toward God, we recognize that He values our growth in character; that we are taking on His holiness and becoming like His Son, Jesus Christ, in our thoughts and actions.

He also values people or characters. He wishes to use us as His instruments to serve people and influence them in a way that will encourage a relationship with Jesus Christ. We are rewarded with joy, purpose and fruitfulness in this life by pursuing these values. And we will be rewarded in eternity.

I can't picture a happier, more blessed life than to know Him personally and to understand and walk in His personal plan for me, drawing the spiritual nourishment from every appointment of every day. If I do that, then I'll grow in character and influence a few characters along the way. God will reward me for wholeheartedly committing myself to His transcendent values.

WORKBOOK SECTION

1
Looking Backward, Inward, and Upward

Proper Foundations • *from Chapter Three*

In our search for truth, we can confuse happiness and joy. Happiness is characterized by luck, good fortune and prosperity. Joy, on the other hand, is a pervasive sense of well-being that we can feel even in the midst of tribulation. It is a word that Jesus used many times.

9. List the circumstances or events in your life that create emotions of happiness and negative emotions (such as anger, fear, depression, etc.). Place a checkmark where you need a Biblical view of joy versus a worldview of happiness.

I feel happy when this happens:

○ _____

○ _____

○ _____

○ _____

○ _____

I experience negative emotions when this happens:

○ _____

○ _____

○ _____

○ _____

10. Put together an action list of what you will do to change those viewpoints that are faulty.

○ _____

○ _____

○ _____

○ _____

11. Character means those qualities that are distinctive to an individual and differentiate that person from others. God promises to reward our pursuit of trying to please Him and take on His character traits. "Being" always precedes "doing." As explained in this chapter, by using the Book of Revelation, chapters 2-4, we can affect the development of our character. Fill in the spaces below to reflect those steps that you must take.

Character trait to be abandoned:

1._____

_____

2._____

_____

3._____

_____

4._____

_____

5._____

_____

Character trait of Jesus to pursue:

1. _____

_____

2. _____

_____

3. _____

_____

4. _____

_____

5. _____

_____

Action steps to take:

1. _____

_____

2. _____

_____

3. _____

_____

4. _____

_____

5. _____

_____

12. As God does something in us to produce character, it naturally spills over into the lives of others, adding characters to His family. Applying the "clock illustration," in the space below, identify individuals in your sphere of influence and an action list of how you could serve them.

Individuals in my sphere of influence:

1. _____

_____

2. _____

_____

3. _____

_____

4. _____

_____

Action list of how I intend to serve each one:

1. _____

_____

2. _____

_____

3. _____

_____

4. _____

_____

SECTION TWO
The Distinguishing Traits of God's Appointments

We are people of destiny, every one of us. Our destiny will be the sum total of God's appointments for us. But what is the nature of those appointments? We need to understand the distinguishing characteristics of God's appointments. Then we can recognize, understand and respond appropriately to the appointments that we encounter in life.

•　•　•　•

"There is a god-shaped vacuum in the heart of every man, which cannot be satisfied by any created thing, but only by God the creator, made known by his son Jesus Christ."

—Blaise Pascal
Physicist & Philosopher

CHAPTER FOUR

Appointments are Born of Grace, Given by Sovereignty, and Nurtured by Free Will

1

Becoming a Thief

As Frederick Buechner says in *The Hungering Dark,* "I believe that by God's grace it is our destiny, in this life or whatever life awaits us, to discover the face of our inmost being, to become at last and at great cost who we truly are." [61]

I think Buechner is saying that God, through His grace, gives us a role in life, then His grace enables us to fulfill that role. He's also saying that this life and the life to come are somehow linked together.

So it is solely by the grace of God that our destinies are born. But what is grace? Grace has profound meaning. As a layman, I could never explain it. Actually, I'm not sure theologians have ever fully explained grace. Grace is mysterious, fully understood only by God.

The word "grace" comes from the Greek word *charis,* meaning blessing or kindness. I once heard a speaker use an acronym to explain grace. He said the letters stood for "God's Riches At Christ's Expense."

As a boy, I had an experience that I think captures the essential nature of grace. I regularly accompanied my mom to her weekly bowling league. The fun part for me was playing pinball machines while she bowled. One night while I was playing pinball, the man who serviced the machines came by to empty the coin boxes. After he left, I noticed he had accidentally left one of the coin boxes unlocked and had forgotten to take out the money.

I cautiously looked around, took the money and bolted for the door before anyone could see me. My pockets were bulging with about $20.00 in dimes. Our house was only a few blocks away, so I hurried home and buried the treasure in my backyard. Then I could just dig them up whenever I wanted to buy something.

I went back to the bowling alley as quickly as possible, so I wouldn't be missed. But when I walked in the door, I was engulfed by guilt. It felt like every eye was focused on me. It was like having a hundred mothers staring icily at you, suspecting you'd done something wrong. I sensed that everyone knew I was a thief.

I began to wonder what would happen if I got caught. There was a reformatory several miles from our neighborhood. Perhaps this was the sort of thing that caused problem kids to be sent to reformatories.

The combination of guilt and fear plagued me for the next hour. I couldn't take it, so I considered my options. I could try to sneak the dimes back into the coin box, but that would be hard to do without being noticed. Or, I could turn myself in. I figured that would mean facing a tribunal consisting of my mom, Mr. Waring, the owner of the bowling alley, and the man who owned the pinball machines. I chose the latter option, hoping to appeal to the leniency of the court.

I started with Mom, thinking she would be most forgiving. Plus, she was friendly with the other two. I knew Mom would be lenient, but I wasn't so sure about them, especially Mr. Waring.

Mr. Waring had a dominating presence. He was tall, quiet and stern. He was the richest man in the neighborhood. In addition to the bowling lanes, he owned the local swimming pool. Talk about power and authority! He could make my favorite places in the neighborhood off limits.

I finally mustered the courage to tell Mom what I'd done, and I could sense her disappointment. She asked what I thought would be the best thing to do. I said I needed to confess my deed to Mr. Waring and return the money.

I was anxious and fearful as we went to his office. However, I was shocked by his response after I confessed and returned the money. He smiled kindly and accepted my apology. He didn't scold me but offered helpful instruction to avoid such situations in the future. *That was grace.*

2
The Consequences—Something I Didn't Deserve

A real surprise happened a few days later when I returned to the bowling lanes with my mom. Mr. Waring saw me and motioned to me. I knew he'd forgiven me, but I was still apprehensive. He asked me to stop by his house after school the next day. I thought: Okay, he's thought about it, and now comes the real punishment. I didn't sleep well that night.

The next day, with some trepidation, I stopped by his home. He invited me in and then excused himself. He came back with a small card, the size of a business card, and gave it to me. I couldn't believe it! It was a one-year free pass to his swimming pool. Summers in Missouri were hot and muggy, so the pass was a treasure. He went beyond forgiving me, which he didn't have to do. He even gave me something extra, at his own expense—something I certainly didn't deserve. *This was another element of grace.*

A special bond developed between Mr. Waring and me. He became my hero and a model of how a man should handle authority and prosperity. His acts were an example of how grace works. God graciously leads us to our appointments in life—not because of our merit but because of His goodness. His grace gives us what we don't deserve and provides ways for us to experience joy, purpose and fruitfulness in life.

It's also God's grace that we can totally blow an appointment, yet He will give us another chance. His grace allows for mistakes. They do not take us out of the game.

Incidentally, there was even more grace in my boyhood story. The man who left the pinball coin box unlocked also forgave me and, ironically, became my father-in-law fifteen years later.

3
Suited to You—an Important Part of Grace

Epictetus, a Greek Stoic philosopher in the first century B.C., made an observation similar to Buechner's. He said: "Remember that you are an actor in a play the character of which is determined by the author—if short, then in a short one; if long, then in a long one. If it be his pleasure that you should enact a poor man, see that you act it well; or a cripple, or a ruler, or a private citizen. For this is your business, to act well the given part; but to choose it, belongs to God." [62]

God casts us in roles that He knows will suit us well. So, like any good actor, we must study our roles. What we will find, perhaps surprisingly, is that God has formed us in such a way that to play our roles well is to be fully ourselves. It would be as if an actor was cast as a particular character, and, as he studied his role, he came to realize that the role was actually like him.

We might not always like our roles, but we must recognize that God has the right to assign roles as He pleases. We must trust Him with our roles. We should then, by an act of the will, be thankful and strive to achieve our full maturity and potential.

> Who are you, O man, who answers back to God? The thing molded will not say to the molder, 'Why did you make me like this,' will it? Or does not the potter have a right over the clay, to make from the same lump one vessel for honorable use and another for common use? [63]

Morgan Freeman, in the movie *Along Came a Spider*, spoke an insightful line. He said: "It's not, 'you are what you do', it's 'do what you are'!" That's good advice.

Much of the unhappiness in life comes from us not being content with who we are, what we look like or what we do. Psychologists, plastic surgeons and employment recruiters must be thankful for this reality. The world certainly evaluates people by superficial measurements. We are prone to compare ourselves to others.

But that is not God's way. Buechner and Epictetus were right. Our roles are born of grace and ideally suited to us. Then our roles, or appointments, are nurtured by the mysterious interplay of God's sovereignty and our free will. But that begs the question: what is God's part, and what is my part?

4
God's Part and My Part
Sovereignty vs free will

Kathy and I recently watched the movie *Open Range,* starring Robert Duvall and Kevin Costner. These two actors play great cowboy roles. We love the direct, non-verbose nature of western dialogue. It drives straight at the heart of truth. But dialogue can also work the other way, reinforcing a lie.

For instance, in one scene Duvall and Costner are standing over two graves they have just dug. One is for Mose, their friend and fellow cowboy. The other is for their dog, Tig. Both were shot by ruthless ranchers in an attempt to force their cattle drive away from the area.

Standing there with hats in hand, they realize that it would be appropriate to offer a prayer. Duvall says to Costner: "If you want to say something to the man upstairs, you go ahead, but I'm not going to talk to [expletive], after what He let happen to Mose." Costner then says a brief prayer and tells God that he's inclined to agree with Duvall, saying that he's going to hold a grudge against Him for allowing this to happen.

This is the great misconception regarding God's sovereignty and man's free will. People want free will. We want to think we can control our lives. Then when people violate and abuse this freedom with an evil act, God gets blamed for it. People wonder how could God allow such a thing to happen. We can't have it both ways.

However, God has ordained that His sovereignty and the free will of man co-exist in a dynamic way. We need to address this dynamic relationship, because our appointments are found in the context of both.

Again, this is one of those mysteries that no one has ever adequately explained. Only God understands the exhaustive truth about the relationship between the two. I can only give illustrations that hopefully provide insight.

For instance, sovereignty and free will are present as I sit here writing. It's early in the morning, and I'm drinking coffee. The law of gravity, which God has ordained according to His sovereignty, is anchoring the coffee cup to my desk. I am free to pick up the cup and take a drink. Gravity is at work, and I am acting within its constraints. But I could foolishly ignore gravity by lifting the cup then releasing it. My blatant misuse of free will and my utter defiance of God's law would result in spilled coffee in my lap. It would be wrong to blame God for something that was obviously my fault.

5
The Ocean Liner Illustration

A. W. Tozer, the famous preacher and author, explaining free will versus sovereignty, said:

> Perhaps a homely illustration might help us to understand. An ocean liner leaves New York bound for Liverpool. Its destination has been determined by proper authorities. Nothing can change it. This is at least a faint picture of sovereignty. On board the liner are several scores of passengers. These are not in chains, neither are their activities determined for them by decree. They are completely free to move about as they will. They eat, sleep, play, lounge about on the deck, read, talk, altogether as they please; but all the while the great liner is carrying them steadily onward toward a predetermined port. Both freedom and sovereignty are present here and they do not contradict each other. So it is, I believe, with man's freedom and the sovereignty of God. The mighty liner of God's sovereign design keeps its steady course over the sea of history. God moves undisturbed and unhindered toward the fulfillment of those eternal purposes which he proposed in Jesus Christ before the world began. We do not know all that is included in those purposes, but enough has been disclosed to furnish us with a broad outline of things to come and to give us good hope and firm assurance of future well-being. [64]

Albert Einstein said: "God does not play dice with the universe." He was acknowledging God and crediting Him for the physical laws of the universe. Isaiah the prophet said much the same but verbalized it differently. He prophesied:

> I am God, and there is no one like Me, declaring the end from the beginning, and from ancient times things which have not been done, saying 'My purpose will be established, and I will accomplish all My good pleasure.' [65]

6

Let's Keep It Clean, Boys

Here is another example of how free will can operate within the constraints of sovereignty. For better or worse, we are a family of perfectionists. I probably shouldn't be, but I'm proud of this trait. Exercising our sovereignty as heads of the home, Kathy and I decree that our home will be tidy. When our sons were little, they didn't share this conviction. They were happier amidst dirt and mud. That didn't matter, because we decreed that our house was going to be clean anyway.

However, because we loved them, we wanted them to acquire this same conviction, believing that they wouldn't be happy going through life perpetually dirty. We embraced a number of strategies over the years to help them develop this conviction. Sometimes we rewarded them with an allowance for keeping themselves and their rooms clean. Other times, we helped them in the efforts, and sometimes we cleaned their rooms ourselves. There were times when it got so out of control that we disciplined them.

Today they are grown men with their own families. It's fun to go to their homes and notice that they, too, have become "neat freaks." The conviction finally became their own. We have to laugh as we watch our grandchildren becoming a third generation of perfectionists.

It reminds me of God's commitment to my character growth. He utilizes a number of means within the context of my free will to move me toward His sovereign goals for my life. Adverse circumstances always have a way of getting my attention, usually the result of my own poor decisions. Sometimes God uses discipline and sometimes love. He uses many things, but ultimately, in eternity, I will be fully developed in character—because He wills it so.

7
Appointments Can Be Written with Pens or Pencils

Historians have posed the question: do people make the events of history, or do the events of history make the person? This is another mind-twisting statement that's difficult to understand. Perhaps both are true—people make history, yet history also makes people.

It's as if God were a cosmic secretary, writing our appointments with pens and pencils. Some appointments in His cosmic day-timer are written in indelible ink. They are unchangeable—things like when and where we are born, our race, our parents and our innate giftedness. Such things flow from His sovereign will and are unalterable.

However, He chooses to write some appointments with a pencil. This gives Him latitude to erase one name and put in another to bring about His sovereign will.

8
A Woman Who Kept Her Penciled-In Appointment

The Book of Esther tells the story of a plot to kill the Jews in roughly 48 B.C. Esther, a Jewish woman who had become queen to King Ahasuerus of Persia, was ideally positioned to plead with her husband to quash a plot being planned by one of the King's court ministers. But she had a choice to make: take initiative or remain silent. Commenting on this decision, Mordecai, one of her chief Jewish counselors said:

> Don't think for a moment that you will escape there in the palace when all other Jews are killed. If you keep quiet at a time like this, deliverance for the Jews will arise from some other place, but you and your relatives will die. What's more,

who can say but you have been elevated to the palace for just such a time as this. [66]

Then, after a three-day period of fasting, she approached the King and pleaded the case of the Jews. She did this at the risk of her own life, for to approach the King was against the law. However, the King reacted positively, and the plot was foiled.

Perhaps at that moment, as God looked down favorably on Esther, He changed this appointment from pencil to ink in His cosmic day-timer.

9
A General Who Affected His Destiny

History is really the record of this relationship between God's sovereignty and man's free will.

There are many instances where people have mismanaged an appointment God had made available to them, thereby affecting their destiny and allowing that appointment to pass to another. Even so, we cannot second-guess God. It is possible that the very act of missing the appointment was part of God's design. We can't know that, only God knows.

The most important thing to understand is that an appointment presented to us is an opportunity that demands our response. To mismanage an opportunity dishonors God and might well compromise our destiny.

One such incident involved General George B. McClellan, who was appointed Commander of the Army of the Potomac in 1861 by Abraham Lincoln. If ever a man was positioned to accomplish something of significance, it was McClellan. The Union desperately needed a man of his stature to lead the military.

The Union forces had been embarrassingly defeated at the First Battle of Bull Run. This was the first major battle of the Civil War and happened just a few miles west of the nation's capitol. So sure of a Union victory at Bull Run, senators and congressmen actually sat on the hillsides to watch the spectacle. Citizens rode out in their buggies with picnic baskets and champagne to see the rebellious secessionists crushed. But it was not to be. The press referred to Bull Run as "the great skedaddle." Over 4,500 soldiers fell that day—hardly a picnic.

Despite the defeat, the North was still vastly superior to the South in terms of resources. They had more finances, supplies, weapons and manpower. Hence, the stage was set for McClellan. By properly utilizing these advantages, he could revitalize the Northern effort.

McClellan recognized the opportunity. Shortly after the appointment, he wrote to his wife: "Who would have thought, when we were married, that I should so soon be called upon to save my country." [67]

After arriving in Washington to confer with Lincoln, he wrote: "I find myself in a new and strange position here. President, cabinet, General Scott and all deferring to me—by some strange operation of magic I seem to have become the power of the land. I almost think that were I to win some small success now, I could become Dictator, or anything else that might please me...But nothing of that kind would please me—therefore, I won't be Dictator. Admirable self-denial!" [68]

However, in the ensuing year, McClellan was indecisive, full of excuses and constantly requesting more resources. Lincoln once quipped: "If I gave McClellan all the men he asked for they could not find room to lie down. They'd have to sleep standing up." [69]

McClellan was forever training but never fighting. Lincoln pressed him to seize the initiative and advance, but the General wouldn't. McClellan wrote to his wife about one such heated exchange with Lincoln: "The President very coolly telegraphed me...that he thought I had better break the enemy's lines at once. I was much tempted to reply that he had better come and do it himself." [70]

He eventually lost all credibility with Lincoln and the Administration. Toward the end of 1862, Lincoln told The White House War Council: "If General McClellan does not want to use the Army, I would like to borrow it for a time." [71] Shortly thereafter, he relieved McClellan of his command. The Northern press jested: "Lee had just lost one of his best Generals."

Using Tozer's analogy, the ocean liner would represent God's sovereign will for a united country. McClellan had the opportunity to play a major role in steering the vessel into its appointed port—a united nation. But he squandered the opportunity. Several other generals succeeded McClellan with the same poor results, until the opportunity fell upon Ulysses S. Grant.

General U.S. Grant demonstrated just the opposite characteristics. He was decisive, strategic and opportunistic. He manifested a dogged determination to see the task through to completion. Grant, through his initiative, claimed the appointment, one that had been available to McClellan.

To reiterate, it would be conjecture at best to attempt to explain fully why McClellan did not seize that historically relevant appointment that God had made available to him. This situation in many ways reminded me of King Saul who also had access to a powerful appointment in life but squandered the opportunity. As a result of his bad judgment and disobedience God ordained that King David eventually replace him.

The prophet Samuel speaks to the situation in I Samuel 13: 13-14:

And Samuel said to Saul, 'You have acted foolishly; you have not kept the commandment of the Lord your God, which He commanded you, for now the Lord would have established your kingdom over Israel forever.

But now your kingdom will not endure. The Lord has sought out for Himself a man after His own heart, and the Lord has appointed him as ruler over His people, because you have not kept what the Lord commanded you.' [72]

What I took away from both McClellan's and Saul's stories was that free will matters. We need to cooperate with God, make wise decisions and respond appropriately to the opportunities before us.

10
Immortality or Purgatory?

I wish I could talk to McClellan. I know how he must have felt. I've made similar mistakes, only in smaller arenas.

One such incident had to do with the not so glorious end to my wrestling career in college. I got to wrestle some of the best collegiate wrestlers in the country. At the big tournaments, I noticed significant differences between us. They had a level of intensity that surpassed mine. In the final analysis, the difference was one of character, not ability.

I felt guilty about this, because I knew I could do better. But I was struggling with the issues from my high school experience. It was a mental trap. On the one hand, I could fully spend myself again and end up being disillusioned, or I could do just the opposite and live with the thought of never realizing or knowing my true potential.

Far and away, the best opponent I ever faced was Dan Gable, probably the most renowned U.S. wrestler ever. He was an incredibly dedicated athlete, clearly out of my league. To my knowledge, he only lost one match in his whole career and later came back to beat that fellow in the Olympic Trials. He was a multiple time national and Olympic champion who went on to captain the U.S. Olympic team. He also won fifteen NCAA Team Titles as the head coach at the University of Iowa. Nine of them were consecutive victories from 1978 to 1986.

I wrestled Gable at the Big Eight Tournament, our conference championship. My coach came into my hotel room the afternoon of the match, put his arm around me and said: "Something's going to happen to you tonight that you'll never forget." What a vote of confidence! I still tease him about what a motivator he was.

I was actually doing well right up till the middle of the second period, when he pinned me. For those not familiar with the sport, that's the worst thing that can happen. It's always humiliating, and, in this case, it happened in front of thousands. If you've ever done something embarrassing in front of lots of people, you'll know how I felt.

Gable went on to wrestling immortality. I went on to wrestling purgatory. I later got injured, and my career slid into obscurity. Purgatory is a state that exists in your mind, where you constantly mumble to yourself thoughts like "If only I could have" or "I should have."

One might well say that it wasn't God's will for me to be a prominent collegiate athlete. And I would agree, but I would add that it would be one hundred percent my fault. I never gave Him a reason to bless the endeavor because of the poor exercise of my free will.

That's not to say that if I'd tried harder it would have guaranteed my success. It wouldn't have. I would have still been limited by other sovereign factors beyond my control, such as God-given ability. But, I would have been a better man, grown more through the experience and enjoyed a clear conscience.

That's my own private little purgatory. Sadly, we can create them in many areas of our lives—and they can't be blamed on God.

11
Be an Initiator

Once during a tour of the U.S. Capitol, I stood on the floor of the House of Representatives and looked up on the wall. There I saw etched in marble a powerful quote by political leader and orator William Jennings Bryan. It said: "Destiny is not a matter of chance, it is a matter of choice; it is not a thing to be waited for, it is a thing to be achieved." [73]

When it comes to the proper exercise of the free will that God ordained, that's good advice. The Bible tells us the same thing. There are times when we need to take action, to do something to effect change.

In fact, Jesus tells us we can know if His Words are really the inspired Word of God or not. He challenges us to discover the truth for ourselves through our actions.

> My teaching is not Mine, but His who sent Me. If any man is willing to do His will, he shall know of the teaching, whether it is of God, or whether I speak from Myself. [74]

In describing this principle, the Bible often uses the word knowledge, or in Greek, *epignosis*. This means experiential knowledge, not head knowledge.

I enjoy the story involving journalist, author and theologian G.K. Chesterton that illustrates the meaning of *epignosis*. During an interview, he was asked: "If abandoned on a deserted island what book would he most like to have with him?"

Chesterton pondered long before giving an answer. The questioner became impatient and offered a few suggestions. Because Chesterton was known for his Christian faith, the interviewer said that perhaps he'd want a Bible. Chesterton's response surprised him. He said: "No, I wouldn't want the Bible. I think I should prefer a good manual on boat building."

God gave us the Bible so that we might discover His truths and apply them to our lives, developing *epignosis,* or experiential knowledge. That's where free will comes into play if we are to properly interact with the sovereign will of God. That's the way to maximize joy, purpose and fruitfulness in life.

WORKBOOK SECTION

2
The Distinguishing Traits of God's Appointments

Appointments are Born of Grace, Given by Sovereignty, and Nurtured by Free Will • from Chapter Four

Our roles are born of grace. God makes places for individuals. He casts us in roles that He knows will suit us well. Our roles, or appointments, are nurtured by the mysterious interplay of God's sovereignty and our free will.

> I believe that by God's grace it is our destiny, in this life or
> whatever life awaits us to discover the face of our inmost being,
> to become at last and at a great cost who we truly are.
> —**Frederick Buechner,** *The Hungering Dark*

13. Do you feel that you are in a role that suits you well, or do you feel you are "out of synch?"

How I feel about my current role in life:

_____

_____

_____

_____

_____

_____

_____

14. God's grace is a foundational aspect of our destiny. From the negative/punishment sense, we do not get what we truly deserve. From the positive/reward sense, we get much more than we could ever deserve.

An experience in my life when I should have been punished but was spared:

_____

_____

_____

An experience in my life when my reward was much more than I deserved:

_____

_____

_____

15. In understanding God's sovereignty and our free will, it is important to see God's part and our part. It is helpful to view our appointments as: 1. Written in pen, flowing from His sovereign will; and 2. Written in pencil and affected by our free will. Fill in the following boxes regarding your pen and pencil appointments.

God has written these things in my life in ink:

_____

_____

_____

_____

God has written these things in my life in pencil:

_____

_____

_____

_____

Here are some appointments in my life written in ink *that I have struggled with:*

_____

_____

_____

_____

16. It is possible to influence our destinies by the actions we take or fail to take.

> Destiny is not a matter of chance, it is a matter of choice; it is not a thing to be waited for, it is a thing to be achieved.
> —William Jennings Bryan

Here is what I'm doing *in my life right now to influence my destiny:*

_____

_____

_____

_____

_____

In light of what I've learned thus far in this book, here are some changes I need to make in my life in order to adequately influence my destiny:

_____

_____

_____

_____

_____

_____

_____

_____

_____

_____

_____

_____

_____

_____

_____

_____

_____

CHAPTER FIVE
Appointments are Infused with Hope and Transcendent Purpose

1
Reaching the Destination

A friend of mine tells a story about an experience he had in the Swiss Alps. It was late spring, and he thought it would be fun to rent a sports car and drive across a winding mountain pass as he moved to his next destination.

When he started out the sun was shining, and the flowers were bursting forth after a long snowy winter. As he continued to climb the pass, he noticed signs written in German appearing every five kilometers. He couldn't read them but could tell they all said the same thing. Each sign had a number on it that was five kilometers less every time a sign appeared (50, 45, 40), etc.

Eventually, he noticed he'd neither passed anyone nor seen any drivers heading back down the mountain. He dismissed this as a bit of good fortune and continued to enjoy the drive.

He became increasingly curious about those signs every time he passed one and was glad when he saw the one with five kilometers on it, thinking he'd soon find out what the big deal was. Shortly, he rounded a curve and saw the road disappear into a massive wall of snow. Then he realized that the signs must have read, "Road closed in 50 kilometers, 45, 40," etc.

His pleasure was quickly replaced by anger and frustration. His hope was dashed. Now he couldn't get to his destination, had wasted a big part of his day and needed to backtrack down the mountain. He chastised himself for being so impulsive and not verifying the route before he departed.

Unfortunately, it's possible to make the same mistake in establishing our purpose in life. We can hit a "massive wall of snow" and lose hope by realizing that, although it was pleasurable for awhile, the way we chose didn't lead us to our desired destination—finding lasting joy, purpose and fruitfulness.

2

Differing Views of Destiny—Ours and His

As I've studied destiny over the years, I've noticed that secular worldviews conflicted with the concept as revealed in the Bible. Secular worldviews typically emphasize prominent positions, status or a notable role in history. Secular worldviews imply that only famous people are people of destiny. The focus is on this world, on temporal life.

Often famous "people of destiny" were aware of their purpose. John F. Kennedy is an example. Shortly before the Cuban Missile Crisis, Mrs. Evelyn Lincoln, the President's personal secretary, found a handwritten note among his papers that said: "I know there is a God—and I see a storm coming; if He has a place for me, I believe I am ready." [75]

I wanted the same thing as J.F.K., to know if God had a place for me. I was pleased to discover that the Bible teaches He does. The prophet Jeremiah said:

> 'For I know the plans I have for you,' says the Lord. 'They are plans for good and not for disaster, to give you a future and a hope.' [76]

However, Kennedy's comment regarding his destiny alluded to a temporal focus—this world. That's typical of a secular view of destiny. But this temporal world is only half of the picture when it comes to the Biblical view of destiny.

According to Jeremiah, God intends that our appointments, or His plans for us, also give us a future and a hope. That hope applies to our life in this world and in eternity—it's transcendent in nature. By transcendence, I mean that purposeful living is meant to affect both temporal and eternal life—the life we know now and the life we will know later.

These differences between temporal views of destiny and the Biblical view have important ramifications. History teaches that when people see their appointments only in light of the temporal, they can end life poorly, disillusioned and bitter—encountering a mental and emotional "massive wall of snow."

I remember once helping a friend go through his father's personal effects shortly after his dad died. Sadly, they did not have a good relationship. I had met his dad shortly before his death, and he came across as a negative, critical individual.

As we sifted through his effects, we found some love letters that he'd written to his wife shortly before they were married. The difference was amazing. The letters were filled with optimism and enthusiasm for life and the future. We couldn't believe the person we knew had actually written those letters. What had happened in fifty years of living that had so drastically impacted him?

The situation reminded me of Philip, the protagonist in Somerset Maugham's novel, *Of Human Bondage,* who visits an aunt and uncle who had helped raise him.

> Philip realized that they had done with life, these two quiet little people: they belonged to a past generation, and they were waiting there patiently, rather stupidly, for death; and he, in his vigor and his youth, thirsting for excitement and adventure, was appalled at the waste. They had done nothing, and when they went it would be just as if they had never been. [77]

Those love letters, like the fictional couple, brought to my mind a great concern—the tragedy of having a wrong worldview of life and ultimately ending life poorly, as if you had never existed. My friend's father, like the Maugham characters, appeared to have become disillusioned with life and ended it on a bitter note.

I've noticed that same phenomenon with various historical figures. Sadly, when their moments on the world stage ended, their joy and purpose ended also. Their gratification had been in the power or fame afforded by their role in life. But, it didn't provide hope and promise for the future when the role ceased to be. However, when I studied people who had a relationship with Christ and shared God's view of destiny, their lives ended on a positive note, even amidst suffering.

Observations from the lives of two historical figures illustrate this point well. Their experiences toward the end of their lives were amazingly similar. Both were plagued by years of physical infirmity, but they responded quite differently.

3
A Hero Whose Life Ended with Bitterness

I've always admired Sir Winston Churchill, who was an incredible leader. He was intimately in touch with his destiny in 1940. In his *Memoirs of the Second World War,* Churchill spoke on the significance of his appointment as Prime Minister: "I felt as if I were walking with destiny, and that all my past life had been but a preparation for this hour and for this trial." [78]

He also sensed his destiny when he was not re-elected in 1945. Speaking about the day of the election, he says:

> …just before dawn I woke suddenly with a sharp stab of almost physical pain. A hitherto subconscious conviction that we were beaten broke forth and dominated my mind. All the pressure of great events, on and against which I had mentally so long maintained my 'flying speed,' would cease and I should fall. The power to shape the future would be denied me. By noon it was clear that the Socialist would have a majority. At luncheon my wife said to me, 'It may well be a blessing in disguise.' I replied, 'At the moment it seems quite effectively disguised.' [79]

Churchill had indeed sensed his destiny. His party was not re-elected. He sensed his purpose in life was finished. It was tied to a position, a title and a role that was no longer his. However, he did serve another term as Prime Minister of Great Britain a few years later. He would live for another twenty years, and for the most part, he did not enjoy them.

Historian Richard Hough writes in *Winston and Clementine—The Triumphs and Tragedies of the Churchills*:

> But as his eighties wore on, the zest diminished and then quite disappeared. Disability followed disability, deprivation followed deprivation. It was a sad decline. At ninety, he had wanted to die ten years earlier. He had long since ceased to paint, and he could not read. Old age had become 'a dreary solitude,' and almost the only emotion he could express was distaste for being alone. [80]

Dreary was Churchill's word for the latter part of his life. Dreariness is exactly the word for a misunderstood destiny. Some of his last words reveal his feelings. To his daughter Diana he said: "I have achieved a great deal to achieve nothing in the end." [81] Just a few days before his death, he spoke some of his last coherent words to his son-in law, Christopher Soames, saying: "I'm so bored with it all." [82] It's sadly ironic that the code name for the committee that handled his state funeral arrangements was "Operation Hope Not."

God intends for our appointments to give us hope for eternity. Randy Alcorn wrote: "You are made for a person and a place. Jesus is the person. Heaven is the place. They are a package—you cannot get Heaven without Jesus or Jesus without Heaven." [83]

When we fail to recognize this, the prospects of retirement, old age and death must be dreary indeed because, without a sense of purpose and a hope for the future, we tend to lose our identity and our sense of individual significance.

I'm not passing judgment on the nature of Churchill's spiritual beliefs. I greatly admire the man. He was perhaps the greatest leader of the twentieth century. We have visited Chartwell, his home south of London, and stood over his grave near Blenheim Palace pondering his life. I'm thankful for how God used him in world events. However, the fact remains that the end of his life was a sad tale. It left me wondering whether or not some of his sadness had been caused by a temporal view of his appointments in life.

4

A Crippled Woman Ends Life with Hope

Contrast Churchill's experience to the end of Amy Carmichael's life. She was a missionary in India for more than fifty-five years, from 1895-1951. During those years, her appointments were dedicated to helping destitute children. Many were rescued from a life of prostitution in Hindu temples. The driving force behind her devotion and sacrificial life was her love for Jesus Christ.

Like Churchill, the last twenty years of her life were years of physical infirmity. In 1931, at the age of sixty-four, she broke her leg, dislocated an ankle and twisted her spine in a severe fall. She never recovered and spent the final years of her life confined to a single room, which served as her bedroom, sitting room and study. During those years she was largely restricted to bed.

After the first three years of this confinement, with little hope of recovery, her doctor told her that she would probably not live longer than five years. In response, her concern was that God would "take from me all slothfulness that I may fill up the crevices of time and truly finish all He wants me to do." [84]

Even at age eighty, bedridden and in tremendous pain, she conducted five hours of interviews daily, wrote books, dictated correspondence and prayed. She also continued to direct the work at Dohnavur, a group of schools, farms and hospitals she had founded.

She never complained. One of her last dictated letters said: "I am very happy and content. Green pastures are before me, and my Savior has my treasure—the DF [Dohnavur Fellowship]." [85]

The end of her life differed significantly from Churchill's. Churchill's comments indicate that he felt his purpose was behind him. He had run into a "massive wall of snow."

However, Amy Carmichael's words reveal that she felt the value and reward for her work was before her. She manifested hope and a sense of transcendence. There was no "massive wall of snow" for her, but rather "green pastures are before me."

5
Part of Hope, Sensing Our Appointments

The hope we receive from sensing our appointments is a wonderful gift from God. It can comfort us during difficult times. Here was one such incident for me.

I have never found transitions to be easy. And as God would have it, my vocational appointments have been in two very diverse fields—healthcare and vocational Christian service. Consequently, transitioning between these two fields of endeavor has always involved some expenditure of emotional energy. I should explain why I have always found moving between those two very different worlds so difficult.

When I was a young man, just out of college I was haunted by the thought of vocational Christian work. It was baggage and the result of faulty thinking. At the time I felt guilty for *not* being a full-time vocational Christian worker. If I really loved Christ, wouldn't I give Him one hundred percent of my time and attention? Why wasn't I a pastor or a missionary or going to seminary? That was valuable work, but other work wasn't, or so I reasoned.

Where does that kind of bad thinking come from? Sadly, it can sometimes come from the pulpit—from bad teaching within Christianity. People can pass along biases that are not Biblical.

That's where it started for me. I was about to graduate from college, and a representative of a non-denominational Christian organization tried to recruit me to join their staff. I was young in my faith and uninformed about most Biblical truths. I had absolutely no appetite for that kind of work. I appreciated the people that did it but thought it wasn't for me. I was interested in law and business.

Then something happened and I will never forget it. We were having a Coke in the Student Union when the person said that if I didn't go on staff for his organization, I'd be running from God's calling for the rest of my life. I would have to settle for a second-class experience with Christ and would limit my ultimate reward in eternity. Although well intentioned, he passed along his bias, and I didn't know enough to realize that his bias wasn't true.

I left that meeting feeling evil, really down on myself. All the things I hoped to accomplish and felt drawn toward now seemed wrong. I felt I must be a bad person for wanting to do them. It was so confusing. Could that be what God's leading was really like? It didn't feel right. But, I looked to this man as a spiritual leader. I assumed that he knew things that I didn't.

Thus was born a two-headed internal monster. One head was my guilt for not being a vocational Christian worker, and the second head was a false view of the merit, honor and legitimacy of any other kind of work.

Consequently, in later years, I could never fully embrace my work. In reality, I did enjoy it but then felt guilty about the enjoyment. There was always the internal monster whispering it was wrong and insinuating that I was running away from God's true plan for my life.

So with a huge load of guilt, I began the initial part of my career in healthcare. That resulted in owning a fairly successful business, as I mentioned earlier, in the field of orthopedics. Those years were, for the most part, years of stability and prosperity. Not only did the business do well, but we had a healthy ministry of evangelism and discipleship with business associates and neighbors, people in our natural sphere of influence.

I did not recognize, however, the natural integration of our spiritual and secular lives. My heart was more and more drawn toward the ministry activities and away from business. Being involved in people's lives, helping them to grow spiritually, was rewarding and satisfying. I felt conflicted between the two worlds.

Then, it happened again, only this time I was being recruited by a different organization and without all the duress. The Navigators, as the name implies, had helped us with our ministry activities, providing needed substance and structure. I appreciated and respected the organization. After working together for several years, they asked us to prayerfully consider joining their staff. I wondered if that move would finally slay the two-headed monster that constantly whispered to me.

I felt both driven and called to this endeavor. I wanted to slay the two-headed monster, and their offer appeared to be the way to do it. So we sold our business and moved to Colorado Springs, the site of their international headquarters.

I will forever be indebted to The Navigators. They taught us much about our faith, and they were used by God to free us from much of our mental baggage. However, although successful from a service perspective, much of the eight-year period was painful and difficult. This was so for several reasons.

First, I totally misunderstood why God had us there. I mistakenly thought this was a lifetime calling, but it wasn't intended to be. It was a time of training and preparation for a later work in healthcare that I couldn't envision at the time.

Secondly, it was meant to be a time of character development, as I learned how to appropriate God's power in my life. God cared more about who I was than what I did. He saw issues in my life that I needed to confront. They had robbed me of joy for years, and I needed to learn how to overcome some bad habits and attitudes. I had thought my time on staff was primarily to help others. But God used it to fundamentally help me.

Finally, it was those eight years that killed the two-headed monster. I had mistakenly thought that I was at last doing noble work, but God used the time to show me that religious work was no more holy than any other kind of work. All work is meant to be holy when properly dedicated to Christ and used for His purposes. I had to experience this for myself to learn that truth.

During those eight years, I developed a growing conviction that I needed to go back into business and put into practice all that The Navigators had taught me. Business was a natural platform for me, and I had access to people who would never go to church, much less search out an organization like The Navigators.

However, my conviction to return to business was accompanied by another issue. If I left the staff, I felt it would be perceived as quitting, and I didn't want to be viewed as a quitter. In reality, this was male vanity and pride. I was blind to the fact that maybe God was leading me back into business. Kathy had sensed this and had been telling me that being a Navigator simply was not me. I was stubborn, however, and wouldn't listen.

I was afraid to talk to anyone about my dilemma for fear that they would think I was abandoning my calling. In fact, one time I ventured into a conversation with a peer about the subject just to see what kind of a reaction I would get, and sure enough, it was the reaction I had feared.

Regardless, I concluded this was a change I needed to make, so I began the difficult transition from the Navigator staff back to healthcare.

The transition began at a meeting regarding my future assignment with The Navigators. Because of my business background, the leadership thought I might be well suited to work in the development department, fund-raising and building relationships for the organization. I had been given a series of psychological tests to help determine if I was suited for the job. The subject of that particular meeting was to discuss the results of the assessment and talk about the position in development.

The meeting was with three senior leaders in the organization. I could sense an air of discomfort. They were all good friends of mine, yet their countenances reminded me of a jury walking back into a courtroom to deliver a guilty verdict. They circulated copies of my test results, which we proceeded to discuss. I'd been recommended for the position, but with a few caveats. In essence, the document said that I was well suited for the position because of my business acumen, but that I really was an entrepreneur and didn't belong in older, mature organizations.

These friends, with heavy hearts, were rebuking me as gently as they could, because they cared for me and wanted me to have a successful career with The Navigators. They implored me to change some characteristics if I wanted to succeed as a vocational Christian worker.

I was rejoicing on the inside as we reviewed the results. I barely heard their rebuffs because I was so excited. I was thinking: Yes, this is me. This is who God created me to be. Don't you guys see it? I was a round peg being squeezed into a square hole.

To my surprise, the Lord used what everyone else thought was a bad thing to actually be a good thing, but only I knew it. All I felt was the love of God. It's as if He were saying: "This is you. Kathy's been trying to tell you this for years. Now I'm telling you. Take action. Run with it. Be fully who I intended you to be."

God's gift of hope made that joy possible. He wanted me to sense my appointment. Hope makes it possible to enjoy watching God custom tailor an appointment just for you, one that will resonate with your spirit and no one else's.

In addition to the hope I felt, I also found the situation to be both humorous and ironic. What was intended as a rebuke and counsel was actually a confirmation of what I wanted to do all along. It was an emotional release that freed me to just be me.

Oswald Chambers said: "I know when the instructions have come from God because of their quiet persistence. But when I begin to weigh the pros and cons, and doubt and debate enter my mind, I am bringing in an element that is not of God." [86]

That quiet persistence had gone on for a long time. This incident convinced me it was time to act. Soon after, I resigned from the staff.

6
Hope Validated

I also validated this change in direction by getting counsel from a number of people I respected. Primary among them was the late Dr. Lorne Sanny, who at the time was President of the The Navigators. He was the successor to the founder of The Navigators, Dawson Trotman, and led the organization for many years.

When I told Lorne my dilemma, he proceeded to encourage me to act on my feelings. He stressed that he thought the greatest need in Christendom was not for more vocational Christian workers but for committed lay people to live by faith in the natural context of life.

He reminded me that one of Trotman's favorite sayings was:

"Never do anything someone else can or will do when there is so much that others cannot or will not do."

He went on to tell me that before he retired from The Navigators, his primary goal was to found a ministry aimed at helping lay people become effective influences for Christ in their careers. This endeavor would be called The Business and Professional Ministry. He encouraged me to go back into healthcare and help with the development of that ministry.

As I pondered the experience, it led me to conclude that God wanted me to sense my appointments. That realization flooded my heart with hope for the future and gave me a sense of His love.

I began to note how scripture affirms God's desire for His people to sense their appointments. God chastised the Israelites for not understanding their times and for not submitting to His plan for their nation.

> For they are a nation lacking in counsel, and there's no understanding in them. Would that they were wise, that they understood this, that they would discern their future! [87]

God's desire had been for Israel to be aware of His purposes for them, to sense their appointments. Their destiny was to model for the world a people rightly related to the Creator of the Universe.

As I meditated on that passage, it was obvious that their refusal both saddened and angered God. Yet this was the very thing I had been doing for years through my erroneous thinking, stubbornness and pride.

So with a renewed sense of purpose, I returned to the business world. However, this time I wasn't filled with confusion, frustration and anger. I was filled with hope and a sense of mission. This was definitely God's appointment for me. I was going back to a job that was just as noble as any other, a job that was ideally suited for me. Finally, the two-headed monster had been slain.

From time to time, especially during periods of discouragement, I pull the psychological assessment from my files and review it. It's now a slightly yellow, twenty year old document. It captures in two brief pages the essence of who God created me to be. It's a reminder of God's love and gives me the encouragement to persevere through difficult times.

7

Hope in the Midst of Darkness

My return to business was marked by surprise and an important lesson, one that demonstrated another distinguishing characteristic of God's appointments.

Although God gives us hope as we sense our appointments, He also wants us to trust Him after the knowledge is imparted. Hence, appointments can be cloaked in adversity, marked by a season of darkness. These periods are intrusions in our lives that often don't make any sense. Such times test our faith and can lead us into a closer relationship with Christ. Isaiah 45:3 says:

> I will give you the treasures of darkness and hidden wealth of secret places, So that you may know that it is I, The Lord, the God of Israel, who calls you by your name. [88]

When I returned to healthcare I was given an opportunity to develop another company in the orthopedic field. I had mistakenly assumed that my business would enjoy the same success as before. I had presumed upon God's blessing. But in reality, we entered into a four-year period of difficulty and pain. The business had changed and all the things that worked well in the past didn't work the second time around.

My presumptions about success soon dwindled away. I felt like I was living under a judgment. It was a test of faith, and I began to question if we were indeed doing the right thing with our lives. If this was the right thing and if it was an appointment from God, then why were there so many problems?

The experience drained us emotionally and financially. I felt we'd been called to that endeavor, but I grew to hate the assignment.

I hoped it would only last for one year, but the struggles lingered on. I was miserable and felt abandoned by God. This situation didn't make any sense to me. I didn't like being perplexed. No matter how hard I worked, we never seemed to get a break. It was one problem after another.

I remember a time about three years into this venture when Kathy came into my office on a Sunday evening. Sundays were always the worst. On Sunday nights I began to dread the week before me, knowing what Monday morning would bring.

She'd been in another part of the house praying about our circumstances and wanted to share some thoughts with me. She proceeded to explain that she felt this would last for another year. That gave me a feeling of discouragement and foreboding. It's the feeling you get when you're surprised by bad news. It reminded me of two situations from my college days. Both of those surprises came in the mail. The first was a notice that my grades for a particular semester were really poor, and the second was orders from the military to report for active duty on my wedding day.

We determined to make peace with the situation and do as good a job as we could with the business. We prayed for deliverance but vowed not to wiggle out of the situation via my manipulation. If deliverance came, we wanted it to be from God, for fear I might get us into something even worse.

As our positive attitudes increased, we began to experience good times in our faith. The pain was real but so was His comfort. God used the suffering to deepen our faith and develop our characters. Happily, it was a time of spiritual unity as we grew closer to each other. Her intuition proved correct. We left that situation exactly one year later.

Those difficult years were a period in my life where I felt most close to God. My feelings for Him were unique. They were like the feelings I had for my dad after he spanked me when I was young. His spankings really hurt but were always followed by his embrace and reminders of his love. I would be sobbing and gasping to get my breath as he held me. It felt comforting to know that he still accepted me and that he cared for me, so much so that he would even hurt me to protect me. Never did the force and presence of a father's love seem more real. Just like my earthly father, God was committed to my ultimate well-being, even if He had to hurt me for a season.

Although I didn't realize it, He used that experience to give me valuable training and character development that I would need for future appointments. In reality, it was a period of blessing. It was a "treasure of darkness."

Psalm 18:28 says: "For You light my lamp; The Lord my God illumines my darkness." [89]

8

The Man Who Always Discerned His Destiny

No life more dramatically demonstrates the possibility of walking in step with God's appointments than the life of Jesus.

Yes, you might say, but He was God—humans could never be that in tune with their destinies. But they can.

When Jesus was twelve, He first exhibited a sensitivity to His appointments. Jesus and His family were visiting Jerusalem to celebrate an annual feast. The family left Jerusalem traveling back to Nazareth in a large caravan.

At the end of the first day's journey, His parents couldn't find Him. He was still in Jerusalem, having recognized one of His appointments. When they returned to Jerusalem, they found Him sitting in the temple listening to the teachers and asking questions.

His parents were upset and scolded Him for treating them in such a way. He responded to them with two questions: "Why is it that you were looking for Me? Did you not know that I had to be in My Father's house?" [90]

His answer shows an awareness of His relationship to His heavenly Father and a sensitivity to His mission in life. It even alludes to a mild rebuff to Mary and Joseph for not recognizing these things.

There is an eighteen-year silence in the Bible regarding the life of Jesus. Then at age thirty, His story proceeds with the start of

His public ministry. This milestone is marked with His baptism by John the Baptist.

As Jesus emerges from the water, a voice comes from out of the heavens saying: "You are My beloved Son and I am fully pleased with You." [91]

What had Jesus accomplished to warrant such an endorsement? All we can ascertain from scripture is that, for the first thirty years of His life, all He'd done was be an obedient son to His parents and labor as a carpenter. God the Father was impressed with who He'd become. Being precedes doing. His obedience and depth of character were what the Father acknowledged.

Then the text goes on to say that He was "impelled" to go into the wilderness to be tested. He was then given the next appointment, one step at a time.

At the beginning of His ministry, He attended a wedding. When the host had run out of wine, Jesus' mother hinted that He should help. He told her: "My hour has not yet come," [92] referring to the appointed time for His public ministry to commence. He knew it was premature to disclose Himself to Israel, especially with a miracle. Nevertheless, He did Mary's bidding, apparently motivated by the love He had for His mother.

The phrase "My hour [or time] has not yet come" is repeated seven times in the Gospel of John. It culminates at the end of Jesus' public ministry. Shortly before the crucifixion, Jesus prayed:

> ...Father, the hour has come; glorify Thy Son, that the Son may glorify Thee, even as Thou gavest Him authority over all mankind, that to all whom Thou hast given Him, He may give eternal life. And this is eternal life, that they may know Thee, the only true God, and Jesus Christ whom Thou hast sent. I glorified Thee on the earth, having accomplished the work which Thou hast given Me to do. [93]

From boyhood to the crucifixion, Christ walked perfectly in step with His appointments. He sensed His appointments. Like ours, His appointments were marked by hope and transcendent purpose. The author of Hebrews tells us: "He was willing to die a shameful death on the cross because of the joy that He knew would be His afterward." [94]

He did experience moments of bewilderment in the Garden of Gethsemane and on the cross, so much so that He asked God why He had abandoned Him. Nevertheless, because of His intimate relationship with the Father, He could say: "I accomplished the work which thou hast given Me to do." He had discerned His destiny.

9
Why Him and Not Me?

I marvel at those references of Jesus being aware of His appointments in life. His example has led me to ask if He could do this, why can't I? Jesus gives us the answer about how we can do this. In John 5:19 He said He only did what He saw the Father doing. It seems to me that He observed what the Father was doing in the following ways. They're easy to list, but hard to practice.

1. *He spent quality time developing the spiritual discipline of studying and understanding scripture.*

2. *He didn't misuse scripture, taking the words and applications out of context.*

3. *He had a disciplined prayer life which He relished because of its deep fellowship and interaction with God the Father.*

4. *He rejoiced in obedience to His Father even when His appointments were painful and unpleasant.*

10
Reviewing the Characteristics

This section has been dedicated to the distinguishing characteristics of God's appointments for us. They are pre-ordained and flow to us from His grace.

Appointments come to us by way of the amazing interaction between His sovereignty and our free will. God's appointments differ from worldly conceptions of destiny because they are infused with hope and transcendent purpose. Nevertheless, there can be periods of darkness. Yet the darkness serves a purpose: It develops faith and character.

And lastly, as we saw from the life of Jesus, God makes it possible for us to go through life sensing our appointments.

2

The Distinguishing Traits of God's Appointments

Appointments are Infused with Hope
and Transcendent Purpose • from Chapter Five

Destiny involves reaching our destination, living a life of significance that will be rewarded in eternity. We can have either a temporal view or a transcendent view focused on the "future hope" of Jeremiah 29:11. As can be seen by the comparison of Winston Churchill and Amy Carmichael, destiny without God is temporal and leaves the deepest yearnings of our hearts unfulfilled. It is rooted in position and power and it changes with circumstances. Destiny with God is rooted in relationship. When circumstances change, core convictions remain. Security and joy come from Whom we know—Jesus Christ—not from what we do.

17. Determine the roots of your perceptions regarding your destiny.

My idea of destiny has been rooted in a relationship with God. Here's why:

_____

_____

_____

Or, *my idea of destiny has been rooted in worldly values. Here's why:*

_____

_____

_____

But, *if my viewpoint was to change and I was to view destiny as rooted in a relationship to God, here is what I would do differently:*

_____

_____

_____

18. God wants us to understand our destiny and has given us Jesus' life as an example. Jesus understood His appointments, as can be seen by the following verses.

> Why is it that you are looking for me? Did you not know that I had to be in my Father's house?   —**Luke 2:49**

> My hour is not yet come.   —**John 2:4**

> Father, the hour has come...I glorified Thee on the earth, having accomplished the work which Thou hast given me to do.
> —**John 17:1-4**

These are some important, positive experiences that have validated what I believe about my destiny:

_____

_____

_____

_____

_____

_____

_____

Even though God wants us to understand our destiny, unexpected circumstances may occur that are confusing and become much clearer with the passage of time.

In evaluating my life to date, I might have misunderstood the following incident or situation and drawn a wrong conclusion about my destiny:

_____

_____

_____

_____

_____

_____

_____

_____

_____

_____

_____

_____

_____

_____

_____

_____

CHAPTER SIX
Appointments Are Revealed in Promises and Commands

1
Camp Faranhyll

We have an annual tradition that we share with friends to welcome the new year. It's unusual, but it's always a big hit. After dark on New Year's Eve, we take guests on an evening snowshoe. We hike to a place we call Camp Faranhyll. This is a quaint, secluded grove of large blue spruce trees on the back of our property.

The hike requires the aid of headlamps, so we can navigate our way through the woods in the dark. This is always perceived as unusual by our guests, who are not in the habit of trudging through snow covered woods at night wearing snowshoes and headlamps.

Then at Camp Faranhyll we build a fire in the middle of the grove of trees and serve drinks and hors d'oeuvres. We enjoy the warmth and glow of the fire for several hours and then snowshoe back home for dinner.

People are always surprised by the ambiance of Camp Faranhyll. The firelight illuminates the giant blue spruce trees and casts beautiful shadows across the snow. Even though it's cold outside, the campfire makes the area surprisingly warm and comfortable. Every year we take many pictures around the fire. These pictures invariably end up on someone's next Christmas card.

Camp Faranhyll doesn't just happen. It has to be created every year and then maintained. First, we have to wait for a couple of feet of snow to fall, which doesn't take long in Colorado. Typically by mid-December, we have enough snow to start packing down a trail, which becomes the pathway to Camp Faranhyll. We call it trailblazing, the strenuous work of tromping down the snow to create the pathway. It can only be done step by laborious step.

Then we have to do the same thing when we get to the site, packing down the center of the grove, so there's adequate space to build the campfire and move around. Originally, we arranged fallen trees in a semi-circle around the fire so people could sit.

We don't just get two feet of snow at our home's elevation of seven thousand feet. Two feet is just the start. So after every snow, the trail and the camp need to be re-packed, and the log benches and tables need to be brushed off. We also gather as much firewood as we'll need and place it all in a storage area we've created to protect it from the snow.

All the effort is well worth it because everyone enjoys the experience so much. Camp Faranhyll started as a unique way to celebrate New Year's. Now it's something we do numerous times throughout the winter, culminating in a "farewell to winter" snowshoe typically in late March.

2
The Pathway Described

The Bible describes a spiritual pathway. And like Camp Faranhyll, if we build and maintain it, it will bring us joy, purpose and fruitfulness. The Apostle Peter described this pathway:

May God bless you with His special favor and wonderful peace as you come to know Jesus, our God and Lord, better and better. As we know Jesus better, His divine power gives us everything we need for living a godly life. He has called us to receive His own glory and goodness! And by that same mighty power, *He has given us all of His rich and wonderful promises*. He has promised that you will escape all the decadence around you caused by evil desires and that you will share in His divine nature. *So make every effort to apply the benefits of these promises to your life.* Then your faith will produce a life of moral excellence. A life of moral excellence leads to knowing God better. Knowing God better leads to self-control. Self-control leads to patient endurance, and patient endurance leads to godliness. Godliness leads to love for other Christians, and finally you will grow to have genuine love for everyone. The more you grow like this, the more you will become productive and useful in your knowledge of our Lord Jesus Christ. [95]

Just like the pathway to Camp Faranhyll is packed down one step at a time, so these elements build on each other, ultimately leading to a mature spiritual life. The path leads from faith to moral excellence to knowing God to self-control to patient endurance to godliness and to love for Christians and everyone. All of these actions involve responding to the promises of God. Hence, we need to address what the promises of God are so we can respond appropriately.

3
An Overview of Promises

Theologians tell us that scriptural promises take three forms: conditional, unconditional and promises of revelation.

Conditional promises have two parts: God's part and ours. In essence, these promises say that if we do certain things, God will do certain things. They also are closely related to the commands in scripture, commands that we need to heed and obey.

For instance, I John 1:9 says: "If we confess our sins, He is faithful and righteous to forgive us our sins and to cleanse us from all unrighteousness." [96] Our job is to fulfill the condition. If we do our part, then God will do His, and consequently our lives are affected. Needless to say, if we do not do our part, i.e. perform the first part of this promise, then our destinies can be compromised.

Unconditional promises, on the other hand, are facts and are based in truth. We can do nothing about them. They simply are. What we can do is rest in them, be at peace and be comforted by their truth.

An example is Hebrews 13:8, which says: "Jesus Christ is the same yesterday and today, yes and forever." While being a statement of truth, it is also an unconditional promise. We can count on the fact that Jesus' character is unchangeable and consistent. He is totally trustworthy.

These types of promises are for all believers of all generations, and their truths provide the framework that shapes our destinies. The first two types of promises are clear enough.

Yet many misunderstandings occur with the third type—promises of revelation. They are given to guide certain people in certain ways at certain times. They deal with the future, that which is unknown. Naturally, this is something we are all curious about. These types of promises, while exciting and powerful, are easy to abuse.

Jesus said: "But when He, the Spirit of Truth, comes, He will guide you into all the truth; for He will not speak on His own initiative, but whatever He hears He will speak; and He will disclose to you what is to come." [97]

It would be nice if the Holy Spirit always provided this disclosure in precisely the same way for everyone, but He doesn't. It would certainly be easier to explain and understand. But then, faith wouldn't mean much. Formulas are not intimate, but personal interactions with the Living God involving His promises are.

Jesus promised guidance into truth and a sense of what is to come. The precise method was never promised. In fact, the Holy Spirit might choose never to lead some people with a promise of revelation from scripture. He is not bound to do so.

I have known sincere and committed Christians who have never had such an experience, yet they are firmly pursuing their appointments in life with conviction. Those convictions were simply given to them in a different manner, one that did not involve a promise of revelation from scripture.

I've also known Christians who felt sorry for themselves or were on some sort of guilt trip because they were never the recipients of such a promise. It's as if this is necessary to validate the Christian experience. It is not. The point is that promises of revelation can happen, and we need to have a general awareness of them so we can respond maturely in the event God ever chooses to guide us in that manner.

4
Conditional Promises:
Focusing on What You Can Control

The Apostle Peter encouraged us to concentrate on the promises of God. He was referring to promises that are always available, i.e. unconditional and conditional promises. Then we need to be diligent to apply them to our lives—hence, obedience. That's something we can control.

I had a significant experience with a conditional promise early in my spiritual pilgrimage. It involved a seminar on prayer, which we attended. Surely, we reasoned, prayer must play a major role in sensing one's appointments in life.

However, I was unaware of a big problem at the time. Further, I didn't understand how the problem was impairing my ability to make any progress regarding my quest for joy, purpose and fruitfulness.

I found the seminar to be frustrating because I wasn't experiencing any of the positive things the speaker mentioned regarding prayer. It was particularly embarrassing to be the one in our group asking all the questions. Obviously, I was the person who didn't get it.

I finally decided to shut up and quit impairing the progress of the discussion group. I'd wait for a more opportune time. After the seminar, I hovered at a safe distance and watched as the speaker received thanks and comments from numerous attendees.

When the crowd started to disperse, I approached and began asking her questions. She instantly sensed my frustration. Being a woman of wisdom and maturity, she knew exactly where to guide the discussion. She asked me if I was harboring any grudges, bitterness or hatred in any of my personal relationships.

I certainly was. I instantly thought about a former business associate who I felt had treated me unfairly. I had angry feelings toward the man and often found myself thinking of ways to get even with him.

His feelings toward me were mutual. We were true enemies, and everyone in our business community knew of the animosity between us. I reasoned that the conflict was a personal problem, and, since everybody has problems, what did this have to do with my prayer life?

Ps 66:18

Then she shared a powerful truth from the Bible, a conditional promise: "If I regard iniquity in my heart, the Lord will not hear." [98]

I was fulfilling the first part of the promise. I was regarding iniquity in my heart. The Lord was fulfilling the other part by not listening to my prayers.

She asked if I was going to change my behavior, so that I could reverse the truth declared by the conditional promise. How I responded would certainly affect the direction of my life. Then she probed further, and I became increasingly uncomfortable. She sensed that I genuinely wanted to live with purpose and please God with my life. She also understood how this situation was keeping me from my objective. Then, she shared the following command from scripture:

not other way around

> If therefore you are presenting your offering at the altar, and there remember that your brother has something against you, leave your offering there before the altar, and go your way; first be reconciled to your brother, and then come and present your offering. [99]

That hurt. But the part that really galled me was the part about my brother having something against me. What about my rights? I felt I had been violated. What about him apologizing to me? I wanted to receive justice, not ask him for forgiveness.

She insisted that I needed to deal with this situation if I wanted to make any progress toward understanding my appointments in life. In fact, she said that this very situation was an appointment, a command to go make the relationship right.

But that was asking too much. I simply couldn't do it. "Okay," she said. "Would you be willing to join me in a prayer asking God to put you in a situation where you would have to deal with this relationship?"

That was disconcerting because I suspected she was the type of person whose prayers God listened to. After all, He had her teaching about the subject around the country.

Now, I hadn't seen my adversary in over a year. So I foolishly comforted myself with the thought that the chances were slim of an encounter between us, and I prayed with the speaker.

I remember quite vividly that the seminar was on a Wednesday evening. I flew out of town on business for the rest of the week. The following Monday something happened that was startling. Evidently, orchestrating a confrontation with my enemy was an easy thing to do for the sovereign God of the Universe. It was a prayer He was happy to answer.

Early Monday morning, I received a page from a customer with an urgent problem. I got to the hospital, rounded a corner, and, to my amazement, I saw my adversary walking toward me from the opposite end of the hall. It was an uncomfortably long hallway. We saw each other and had lots of time to ponder the impending confrontation.

But something powerful happened, an experience I'll never forget. I instantly thought of the seminar and the prayer. I realized I was dealing with a supernatural situation, or, better yet, an appointment that was meant to be uniquely mine.

I shot off a quick prayer begging for the strength to do the right thing. I was convinced it wasn't within me to ask forgiveness from a man I resented; one whom I thought should be apologizing.

Then, the miracle happened. I experienced a sensation of the hatred and anger leaving me.

As we approached one another, I quickly said that we needed to talk and that I'd like to apologize for all the animosity between us. I couldn't believe my words. It happened so quickly, but there the words were, out there: "would you forgive me?"

His response wasn't as gracious. He cursed me. However, his words seemed to bounce off, as if a shield was in front of me deflecting the hurt his words were intended to cause. All I felt was compassion as I saw his anger. I marveled about how, at that very moment, I was being freed from my own anger.

God in His love released me from the burden of those damaging emotions. Evidently, my character development was more important to God than the loss I had incurred as a result of this man's actions.

In the years that followed, our paths crossed several times. Each time the confrontations were less intense. In fact, the last time I saw him the exchange was cordial.

5
Promises and Commands: Known vs. Unknown

The experience taught me about the close and important link between the promises and commands of God. Both are known entities. They are revealed plainly in scripture. Just like each step compacting the snow creating the pathway to Camp Faranhyll, so obedience to God's promises and commands form the pathway by which we discover our appointments that ultimately make up our destinies. In reality, our actions of obedience are our appointments.

At that time, my propensity was to be more drawn toward the unknown. By that, I mean the fascination, curiosity and intrigue of what the future would hold for me. I looked for signs and conjured up mystical interpretations for various events in my life. It was as if the world revolved around me and my need for self-realization. I was totally preoccupied with myself. In actuality, I'd gone to that seminar to see if I could use prayer to get God to tell me what was planned for my future. Prayer for me was really just another spiritual tool I could use to construct my narcissistic kingdom of self.

I was focused on the third type of promise, promises of revelation. I wanted God to tell me about my future. What I wasn't prepared to do was respond in obedience to a command in scripture that was closely linked to a promise. I especially didn't want to be obedient in that situation because it meant enduring the humiliation and emotional pain of apologizing to a person that I detested.

But in doing so, I had a wonderful experience with God. I sensed His invisible orchestration of the appointment. I felt His power enabling me to respond appropriately, something that I knew was beyond my personal capacity. I learned that forgiveness feels better than hatred, and that it's worth dying to self to enjoy a forgiving spirit.

I learned that God's way of dealing with life's situations is always the best way. Obedience took me to a better place, a place where I had an increased capacity to experience joy, purpose and fruitfulness—the very things I craved.

My faith was bolstered that day. I became even more convinced that, although He is invisible, He is nonetheless real. I moved from being what I call "a believer/hoper" to becoming "a knower."

When I was a little boy, we lived in a home with an archaic charcoal heating system. I remember my dad telling me to watch out for the heating grates in the floor. "They are hot and will burn you," he said. I believed him, but not with much personal conviction. Then, one day, I purposely touched a grate. I came away with a painful burn on my hand that looked like the marks on a steak fresh off the grill.

At that moment I moved from being "a believer" to being "a knower." I'd had my own experience with the hot grates, and now my convictions were personal, real and strongly felt.

6

Unconditional Promises: Paying Attention to Truth

Some things in life are just true. Recognizing and responding to truth can greatly affect our destiny. These truths are often stated as unconditional promises in the Bible. They are statements of fact upon which we can build our lives.

I have a favorite story dealing with such promises. I am especially fond of it because it involved two of my favorite people, my wife, Kathy, and son, Matthew. The incident changed how I reacted to my future appointments in life.

It was about the same time as my experience with the prayer seminar and my confrontation with my business adversary. During those days, we held Bible studies every Friday evening in our home. The attendees were neighbors and business associates we had befriended.

One night after the study, I was talking with a wonderful fellow named Tom, who's still a dear friend. He was a business associate who'd invited to the study. It was early in the spiritual pilgrimages for both Tom and his wife Sherry, and the sessions were having a big impact on their thinking.

I was rather proud of this fact and asked him what it was that was affecting him. Secretly, I was trying to draw a compliment from him, seeking praise that would gratify my ego, fulfilling my need for approval from others. I was thinking he would surely mention the many Biblical truths I pontificated on.

However, that wasn't Tom's response. Tom's a wise man and he always was. So, he thoughtfully considered my question and proceeded to say that it was the warmth, comfort and love that he felt in our home. He then proceeded to gush forth compliments about what a hostess Kathy was. I appreciated all the nice things he was saying about my wife but was inwardly humbled and felt rebuked because of my attitude. It wasn't the response I was expecting.

What he was feeling was the love of Jesus Christ that radiated from Kathy's character, personality and gift of hospitality. Kathy, in her humble service, gave Tom something my teaching was powerless to provide. He went on to say that the atmosphere in our home was what he and Sherry craved for their home.

They went on to create just that. Over the years, their home has been a haven for many. They would probably tell you that they first saw that modeled for them by Kathy.

But the encounter with the unconditional promise happened a few days later as I was reading in the Book of Proverbs. I was stopped dead in my tracks by Proverbs 29:23 which says: "Pride ends in humiliation, while humility brings honor." [100]

It wasn't a command to be humble or to avoid pride, although the Bible teaches that. It was simply stating a truth. God has promised that pride and humiliation will accompany each other, as will humility and honor. I realized that my life was reflecting the former and Kathy's the latter. I needed to reflect on that truth, which was also an inevitable promise, and change my behavior. Otherwise, I was certain to adversely affect my destiny, not to mention bring a lot of heartache to God, the lover of my soul.

However, I didn't react to that unconditional promise appropriately. I got down on myself for harboring so much pride in my heart.

It took another encounter with an unconditional promise to pull me out of the spiritual tailspin, and that involved my son Matthew.

Early in the morning of the next day, I was reading in the Book of Micah. Matthew was about four and had just gotten up. Usually, he made a beeline for either the television to watch cartoons or the breakfast table to eat. But that morning, he came downstairs into my office and lay down on a rug in front of our fireplace. He lay there sucking his thumb by the glowing fire, as he clutched his favorite blanket and stared at me.

My heart melted. He looked so cute, innocent and vulnerable. I was filled with thoughts of love for him and of what a blessing he was. Then I heard a voice in my head say: "That's how I feel about you, Bill. You're my son. I love you in the same way you love Matt." God used this very real and personal analogy to teach me a great truth and to snap me out of my discouragement.

I was overcome with emotion as I reflected on how much I loved Matt. For me, to be a father is one of life's richest treasures. Could that possibly be how God feels about us?

I joined Matt on the rug and held him tenderly, savoring the moment. Then, he went upstairs, and I returned to my desk. As I resumed my reading, once again I was stopped dead in my tracks. As if the experience with Matt wasn't enough, God in His graciousness proceeded to explain His heart to me via the last few verses in Micah.

Once again You will have compassion on us. You will trample our sins under Your feet and throw them into the depths of the ocean! You will show us Your faithfulness and unfailing love as You promised with an oath to our ancestors Abraham and Jacob long ago. [101]

Contextually, these were unconditional promises for the Israelites. However, Paul, throughout the book of Romans, makes the point that they are also promises for Gentile believers as well—people like me.

God unconditionally promised to trample my sins under His feet and to be faithful to me and love me with an unfailing love. That was simply true. I could do nothing about it. It just was. I could rest in these truths. I could let them fill my heart with comfort, and I could quit wallowing around in self-pity.

To this day, one of the fundamental anchors in my life is my confidence in God's unfailing commitment to me as my Father. In spite of my failures and sinfulness, I believe He will always be there for me, just like I aspire to be there for my boys.

This truth has reinforced my commitment to Christ during difficult times. It's hard to turn your back on someone if you know they are unconditionally committed to you. The reality of it has guided my responses to many of life's appointments, thereby affecting my destiny.

7
Dealing with Promises of Revelation: Isaiah 61

In Chapter Five, I told a story regarding the initial transition we made from business to vocational Christian work. There was another aspect to that story that I saved for this chapter, namely that God sometimes sheds light on our appointments through promises of revelation revealed in scripture. God gives promises of revelation to some Christians on a "need to know basis," if He thinks it's necessary to guide and encourage them. There was such a situation for me.

It's a common thing for people to have days when they are frustrated with work. Actually, if others are like me, they have days when they feel trapped, bored and frustrated, struggling to see the purpose in their lives. On days like that I think the only reason for work is money. I have responsibilities and people to care for.

What I really long for is work that will consume me in a positive sense, that engages my passion and causes me to fully spend myself. I'd like work that affects people now and long after I am gone. I want work that validates my existence.

I clearly remember a frustrating day in the fall of 1976. It was a beautiful October day in Denver. The sky was incredibly blue, and the first dusting of snow for the season was on the mountains. I had slipped away from work and gone to a driving range to take out my frustrations on golf balls. Things were beautiful on the outside but ugly on the inside, as I pelted the balls.

This was before the two-headed monster had been slain, and it was at work in my thought life. It gnawed on my mind with a lingering thought: surely I was meant to do more with my life. I'm capable of doing more. What if this was all there ever was for me to do? What if this was my life? The thought frightened and sickened me.

The irony was that things were going really well. My business was doing well. We were getting ahead financially. I liked my business associates and customers. However, I wasn't fulfilled, and I couldn't shake the idea that I was created for something else, something special. If I wasn't, then I drastically needed to change my perspective regarding my work. I needed to understand what was special about it. Otherwise, I was in for some unhappy years.

How do you shake off days like that? Usually, I couldn't. I simply endured them, and eventually I would start to feel better. But later that day, I had an experience that jolted me out of the despondent mood, an experience that replaced my despondency with hope. I had an encounter with a promise of revelation.

At that time in my life, I tried to spend a small amount of time by myself at the end of every day. When I got home, I would immediately go to my study and read scripture. This had the effect of decompressing me from the events of the day, refreshing me and reorienting me toward focusing on my family for the evening.

I had been working my way through the book of Isaiah and came to chapter 61. This chapter starts with prophecies about Jesus and His ministry. Then the text transitions and describes distinguishing characteristics that mark the lives of people who have been touched by Christ. It said they would be "planted" or placed by Him so their lives would bring Him glory (verse 3). I was particularly drawn to verses 4-9, especially verse 6:

> But you will be called priests of the Lord; you will be spoken
> of as ministers of our God. You will eat the wealth of nations,
> and in their riches you will boast. [102]

I was mesmerized by this verse. It seemed in some way to speak to the inner conflict I was experiencing regarding my work. In my thinking, the first half of the verse alluded to vocational Christian service. That was something I was contemplating, just walking away from business and becoming some sort of minister. Yet the second half of the verse reminded me of business, "eating the wealth of nations."

The question was how to weave the two very different worlds into one. This was at the heart of my conflict. I had never been able to reconcile these two worlds, and I simultaneously yearned to live in both. Yet they were very separate worlds and were by no means integrated in my life experience.

I had a Christian life that was comprised of church attendance, Bible studies, socializing with Christian friends and saying grace before meals. Then I had a Monday through Friday business life, full of pressures and issues that were anything but Christian. Nary did the two worlds meet, and that was the essence of my frustration.

How could I extract spiritual meaning from all those hours spent in the marketplace? How could I integrate those two worlds into one? I was tired of my dualistic lifestyle. I wanted one life and one purpose.

Isaiah 61:6 somehow spoke to that mystery. To loosely paraphrase what I felt, it's as if God was saying to me: "You will be thought as a minister, but, by the way, you're to eat the wealth of nations. The essence of your life will center on reconciling these apparently two disparate worlds. You will minister for Me in the marketplace. I assign spheres of influence. Just like I sent Peter to the Jews and Paul to the Gentiles, you're being sent to the healthcare marketplace."

Contextually, I realized that these verses literally applied to the nation Israel. But my heart was quickened by the thought that God had chosen to use them in a personal way in my life. Somehow, they spoke to my situation. It's as if the words were blinking in neon in my mind's eye.

God must have sensed that I needed that type of guidance and encouragement, because hope instantly replaced my sense of vocational depression. I had no idea how any of this would happen, but I had a sense that I was about to embark on a journey of discovery and purpose. My view of work began to change that afternoon.

Those few verses in Isaiah have acted like a rudder on a ship, providing direction and stability for my family and me as we have interacted in the two worlds of vocational Christian work and business. For over thirty years, every vocational decision we've made has been analyzed in light of the decision's practical fulfillment of what we believe those verses mean for our life's purpose.

We are still making wonderful discoveries about how our business life is really a calling from God. We've been given relationships with many wonderful people, people who will never step into the Christian world. Our job has been to try to take Christ to them, to befriend them, serve them and pray for them.

Over the years, all my business experiences have been powerful tools to change me, to create growth and nurture spiritual substance. I have failed much and often, but I've always learned. I've felt that when I walked into a corporate headquarter or a hospital, I was really walking into a ministry experience intended for me. I wasn't walking into a drab business experience. Work has been full of spiritual purpose.

8

Wishful Thinking or True Promises?

Guidance for our destinies often comes to us from scripture by way of the revelatory promises of God through the promptings and leading of the Holy Spirit. We must believe them by faith, and then they are confirmed by circumstance.

However, these types of promises can be problematic. It's easy to abuse or misuse these types of promises. Often what someone believes to be a promise of God is in reality wishful thinking stemming from wrong desires.

If we feel we have received such a promise, how can we make sure it's not wishful thinking? Wishful thinking centers on what we want. Authentic promises from God center on what He wants—for us to mature spiritually and to bear fruit for His Kingdom.

I like a story from Abraham Lincoln's life that addresses this issue.

One day during the war, a minister said to Lincoln that he hoped "the Lord is on our side," to which Mr. Lincoln replied: "I am not at all concerned about that, for I know that the Lord is always on the side of the right; but it is my constant anxiety and prayer that I and this nation should be on the Lord's side." [103]

A friend of mine told me an amusing story that further illustrates this point. Early in his life he was involved in a ministry focused primarily on young people. One of the participants was a beautiful girl who caught the attention of all the guys. Three young men were especially attracted to her and pursued her. After a while, all three sought counsel regarding the girl with an adult leader of the ministry. Ironically, all three presented what they believed were legitimate promises from God. Each was convinced that this young woman was God's woman for him.

We know that God can't lie, so who was right? Several years later, she did indeed marry one of the three. What the other two thought were promises from God were no more that wishful thinking and youthful lust.

Some people's faiths can get totally shipwrecked because they believe God promised something and didn't deliver. In reality, this is always faulty thinking.

An incident from the life of the Apostle Paul is an example of an authentic promise of revelation. Early in his first missionary journey, he directed the primary focus of his work toward Jews. Later, he changed that direction to focus primarily on Gentiles. In doing so, he said in Acts 13:47: "For thus the Lord has commanded us, 'I have placed you as a light for the gentiles, that you should bring salvation to the end of the earth.'" [104]

Contextually, this was a prophecy about Jesus as recorded in Isaiah 49:6. However, as Paul read Isaiah, the Holy Spirit impressed his spirit that it also disclosed the future, giving specific direction to his ministry. Again, he was the only man that had that particular experience. Evidently, in the wisdom of God, it was appropriate for Paul at that moment. By looking at other parts of scripture, we see that this was verbally directed by Jesus (Acts 9:15), then affirmed by the counsel and advice of other apostles and validated by circumstances as his missionary journeys evolved.

A friend of mine once told me a story that has stuck with me through the years. He is a physician and mentioned that he'd had a marvelous experience during his residency training in Florida.

His mentor through his training was a Christian man who he truly respected because he conducted his medical practice in a manner that reflected his values and beliefs. This was particularly appealing to my friend and his wife, so when the man asked him if he would stay and join the practice, it was an offer that they found very enticing. But for some reason, they couldn't quite bring themselves to the point of accepting.

They spent a good bit of time praying for direction. Then one day while reading his Bible, my friend said he was strangely affected by a passage in Romans. The Apostle Paul said: "And thus I aspired to preach the gospel, not where Christ was already named, that I might not build upon another man's foundation." [105]

It struck my friend that this is exactly what he would be doing if he stayed in Florida, building on another man's foundation. He sensed it wasn't for him. With a bit of sadness, but also anticipation for the future, he declined the offer and headed back to his native South Dakota.

They've been there ever since and have not only established a fine medical practice, but have also created a strong and powerful Christian influence in their community. For thirty-some years, they've been building on their own foundation. Their appointment was revealed to them supernaturally under the guidance of the Holy Spirit.

And your ears will hear a word behind you, 'This is the way, walk in it,' whenever you turn to the right or the left. [106]

9
Twisting Promises

It seems to me that my physician friend had a legitimate experience with a promise of revelation from God. He was given specific direction from a passage in scripture. This prompting was only for him at that moment in time. Its authenticity has been validated by years of fruitfulness. However, it's not always so.

Unfortunately, for every positive story, I can recall numerous stories that didn't have happy endings. I know people who were convinced that God had guaranteed them a child or a certain mate or a job or some material possession. Once we saw someone abandon a mate who had acquired a debilitating disease. That person decided to marry someone else, saying that Jesus had promised abundant life, a perverse twist of John 10:10.

What do such stories have in common? They tell of people who abused and misunderstood the promises of revelation from God.

10
So What's the Bottom Line?

This chapter has not been an exhaustive treatment of this complex subject of God's promises, but hopefully it has provided enough insight to protect and guide us as we try to decipher and understand our appointments in life.

The following list may not necessarily be theologically correct, but it is a practical tool I've developed to help me contemplate a potential promise from God that could affect the direction of my life. I ask myself—does the promise **always** do certain things and inversely **never** do certain things? It's my hope that this list will be a guide post for stories with happy endings.

- Real promises are **always** intended for God's glory, **never** ours.

- Real promises are **always** meant for our spiritual well-being, **never** our comfort.

- Real promises are **always** meant to bear fruit for His Kingdom, **never** for our kingdom.

- Real promises are **always** confirmed by godly counsel and should **never** be acted on in a spirit of independence.

- Real promises are **always** consistent over time. They **never** vary.

- Real promises are **always** given to protect us and help us endure life's struggles. They are **never** for our perceived convenience.

- Real promises should **always** be accepted by faith, **never** wavered on in a spirit of doubt and instability.

- Real promises might not **always** come true in your lifetime, but they will **never** fail.

- Real promises are **always** given for our encouragement, **never** for feeding our fears and insecurities.

- Real promises will **always** be about Jesus Christ and your relationship to Him. They will **never** be only about you.

2

The Distinguishing Traits of God's Appointments

Appointments Are Revealed in Promises
and Commands • from Chapter Six

Our spiritual pathway is built on the solid foundation of God's promises. Scriptural promises take three forms: conditional, unconditional, and revelational. Guidance for our destinies is announced to us from scripture by the promises of God, through the prompting and leading of the Holy Spirit. We must believe them by faith; then they are confirmed by circumstances.

19. Conditional promises have two parts: God's and ours. If we do certain things, then God will do certain things. As mentioned in this chapter, these promises are often tied to commands.

What are actions you have been convicted to take as a result of recognizing a conditional promise of God?

_____

_____

_____

_____

_____

_____

_____

_____

20. Unconditional promises are facts and are based in truth. We can do nothing to alter them.

What are some unconditional promises that you need to believe and rest in?

_____

_____

_____

_____

_____

_____

21. Revelational promises are given to guide certain people, in certain ways, at given times and involve the future or that which is unknown.

Do you feel that you have been given a revelational promise from scripture and has it been validated by counsel and circumstances?

_____

_____

_____

_____

_____

_____

_____

CHAPTER SEVEN

Appointments and Spiritual Chain Reactions:
Obedience, to Power, to Unique Character

1

An Explosive Power

My first experience with gunpowder wasn't pleasant. But it did leave a lasting impression.

I was about seven. We were celebrating the Fourth of July at my grandparents' home. My cousin and I were exploding firecrackers in their front yard. He lit one and threw it. Being a typically uncoordinated little boy, he accidentally tossed the sparking missile my way. It was about four feet from my left ear when it exploded.

Two things quickly happened. One, he got in lots of trouble, and two, my hearing became impaired for life.

Firecrackers were more powerful back then. But still, it was just a firecracker. Can you imagine the explosive power of dynamite?

Yet that is the word God chooses to describe His power operating in our lives. The Greek word for power is *dunamai*, from which our word dynamite is derived. So when God speaks of His power operating in your life, He has something powerful in mind. The pathway described by Peter in the last chapter (II Peter 1:2-8) started by saying: "…His divine power gives us everything we need for living a godly life."

My cousin started a chain-reaction with that firecracker. He lit it and tossed it. Then it exploded and I was permanently affected. In life, as we live obediently, a spiritual chain reaction occurs. God's Spirit works within us to create power. That happens because His truths are powerful. We experience an explosion, an explosion of character.

As we apply His truths to our lives, we change and become more stable and consistent in our behavior. We become stronger people, men and women of deeper character. Deep character is powerful, and it positively affects our destiny. Therefore, obedience produces power, and power produces character. Finally, character impacts destiny. Also, as I mentioned in Chapter Three, character is something God has promised to reward in eternity.

The spiritual chain reaction is not a trite Christian formula. It's simply true. We've all met people with character shaped by God. They are people with spiritual authority. Their life reflects a demeanor or presence that commands respect. They are people who influence others.

Jesus manifested those qualities of spiritual authority and personal presence. It was said of Him that "…He was teaching them as one having authority, and not as the scribes." [107]

The fundamental issue is whether or not we will obey, thereby allowing God to create this spiritual power in us. If we do obey, we will have a significant destiny and experience joy, purpose and fruitfulness.

Disobedience, on the other hand, creates a chain reaction that works inversely. It robs us of power and spiritual authority, thereby compromising destiny. It prevents us from realizing God's highest and best for our lives.

This principle is clearly evident in life. It's hard to watch an evening newscast that doesn't feature an example of a person with a warped worldview who has disobeyed the law and exerted a negative influence on society. Disobedience produces a life of no eternal value. Jesus said: "Either make the tree good, and its fruit good; or make the tree rotten, and its fruit rotten; for the tree is known by its fruit." [108] His statement leaves the "making" part up to us. Oswald Chambers, in *My Utmost for His Highest,* speaks to this issue. He says:

> We are in danger of forgetting we cannot do what God does, and that God will not do what we can do. We cannot save nor sanctify ourselves—God does that. But God will not give us good habits, or character, and He will not force us to walk correctly before Him. We have to do all that ourselves. [109]

2
Unique Character Traits Mark Destiny

I mentioned that the exploding firecracker left me with a lasting impression. By that, I mean more than just the impaired hearing. I personally felt the effects of the power. It created in me a strong conviction regarding how to handle explosive things such as firecrackers, guns and flammables.

Similarly, as we obey, we feel the powerful effects of God's truth at work in our lives as our convictions develop. These are God-inspired convictions that move us to live a certain way. Over a lifetime, they become the distinguishing character traits that mark our lives and destinies. They become a central part of our life's message.

We are all developing distinguishing character traits that are unique to us. We hear them all the time, comments like "she's so kind-hearted" or "he's really conscientious about his work." Over time, we become known almost exclusively by those traits. If you want to get a sense of how your personal destiny will be characterized, take a look at those traits. How do people describe you?

And it doesn't end when you die. In fact, these unique qualities especially crystallize after death. History remembers people by their unique traits. Ronald Reagan was "The Great Communicator." Lincoln was "the Great Emancipator." Washington was "Father of his Country." Your life too will be summarized by your traits. Think about it: eulogies are typically a recitation of the positive traits that were evident in a person's life.

In the last chapter, I told the story of my friend Tom associating hospitality with Kathy. If you ask any of our friends, "When you think of Kathy, what comes to mind?" I believe they would all comment on what a gracious hostess she is.

Having dated Kathy for forty years, I've been there to see how this conviction developed. As a girl, her parents spoke often about the importance of hospitality and always modeled hospitality in their home. Plus, they also taught Kathy how to cook, serve and be a gracious hostess. She experienced the joy of a hospitable home and witnessed the effect gracious acts had on others. She in essence felt the power and truth of hospitality. As a young woman she saw in scripture how God commanded hospitality (Hebrews 13:2, Romans 12:13, I Timothy 5:10).

All of this created conviction in her life regarding the value and importance of hospitality. It became a distinguishing characteristic that marks her life. It's been fundamental to our marriage, family life and Kathy's destiny.

We believe that hospitality is a gift from God, intended for use in a positive way to influence others. Consequently, we try to stay sensitive to opportunities to be hospitable, believing they are appointments from God. We feel that hospitality is a stewardship that has been entrusted to us, and that, if we are conscientious, one day we will be rewarded in eternity.

3
Studying Models: An Illustration from History

One of my favorite historical figures is Robert E. Lee, the great Civil War general. In analyzing and commenting on Lee, historians invariably mention a distinguishing trait of his life—his sense of duty.

Those under his command often referenced it as well. One officer, writing after his service with Lee, said: "Duty first, was the rule of his life, and his every thought, word and action was made to square with duty's inexorable demands." [110]

Lee himself once wrote: "There is a true honor, the glory of duty done, the honor of the integrity of principle." [111]

But how did this conviction develop in his life? That's the interesting point. We are well served to pay attention, because we all have situations evolving in our lives that will develop traits that are unique to us. Those traits will become the distinguishing elements that will mark our destinies. Studying Lee's story will help us recognize this same process at work in our lives.

4
Models Are There, Both Good and Bad

God uses people and circumstances to provide models for us. We look to our models for guidance. As a result, we develop convictions. If it's a positive model, we emulate it. If it's a negative model, we avoid it and are motivated to do just the opposite. It's modeling either way, and we are affected.

My in-laws provided a positive model of hospitality for Kathy. However, Robert E. Lee's sense of duty was created because of a negative role model that seriously impacted his life.

His father, Lieutenant Colonel Henry Lee, better known as "Light Horse Harry," was a brilliant military strategist and cavalry commander for George Washington during the Revolutionary War. Cornwallis' surrender to Washington at Yorktown, Virginia, effectively ended the war. It was the elder Lee's plan that lured Cornwallis to that fateful place.

"Light Horse Harry" became a prominent figure after the war. He was a member of the Continental Congress, elected Governor of Virginia and was spoken of as a potential future President. He gave the eulogy at Washington's funeral and coined the phrase that still evokes the legacy of our first President: "First in war, first in peace, and first in the hearts of his countrymen."

Unfortunately, he also had character flaws. Twice he married wealthy women and squandered their fortunes on risky financial ventures. The second woman, Anne Carter, was Robert E. Lee's mother and rumored at the time to be one of the wealthiest women in colonial Virginia. He was known as a profligate womanizer who spent money recklessly. Twice his actions landed him in debtors' prison.

Beaten down by circumstances that he created, the elder Lee abandoned his family and went to the Caribbean. He wandered about aimlessly for six years and finally died there. Young Robert was six when his father left and twelve when his father died.

In Henry Lee's life, we see the negative chain reaction illustrated: disobedience prevents one from living powerfully, diminishes spiritual authority and renders personal influence that is negative. Sadly, there is no evidence of fruit being generated that would merit reward in eternity.

I wonder if Henry Lee was experiencing joy, purpose and fruitfulness while wandering aimlessly around the Caribbean waiting to die. He was a man who did not fulfill his duty to anyone around him, most importantly to those people for whom he was personally responsible. Robert E. Lee must have experienced much pain resulting from his father's actions.

To further complicate things, his mother became an invalid. The situation demanded duty. Lee became both her caregiver and the manager of the household. He would be seen around Alexandria, Virginia, carrying his mother in his arms, moving her from chair to coach as they ran errands. Toward the end of her life she said: "How can I live without Robert? He is son, daughter, and everything to me!" [112]

Shortly after his mother's death he had another experience that would further deepen his convictions regarding duty. He married Mary Randolph Custis, the great-granddaughter of George Washington. One historian said: "This marriage, so I think, had a marked moral influence on him, for in the eyes of the world it made him the representative of the family which had founded American liberty.... More than ever he now had a reputation to live up to—the reputation of Washington—and from that day onwards he became his representative on earth." [113]

5
Lee's Biggest Sacrifice for the Sake of Duty

Many of our vacations are pilgrimages in search of insights into destiny. We like to go to places where momentous events occurred, in history or in the life of an individual. Insights are powerful when you're actually standing where someone experienced a significant appointment.

Arlington National Cemetery is such a place. It sits across the Potomac River from Washington D.C. Most people go there to pay homage to John F. Kennedy and reflect on that terrible day in

November of 1963. Older adults can tell you exactly where they were on November 22.

However, sitting directly above Kennedy's grave is an equally mesmerizing place, the Custis-Lee Mansion. This beautiful plantation had been the home of Robert E. Lee's father-in-law, George Washington Parke Custis. He was referred to as the "child of Mount Vernon" and the adopted son of George Washington.

After the marriage, the mansion became Lee's home as well, and he lived there till the outbreak of the Civil War. Unlike his father, who had effectively lost his family's plantation, Lee was an excellent steward of the mansion and loved the place.

It was here that he agonized over the role he should play in the coming conflict. As we toured the mansion and walked around its beautiful grounds, it was easy to imagine his agony. Surrounding him at Arlington were the many family relics from George Washington. Married to Washington's great-granddaughter, Lee was son-in-law to Washington's adopted son. He was in effect Washington's heir.

Further, Lee was a distinguished soldier. He had been the only cadet to go through West Point Military Academy without receiving a single demerit, and he had gone on to be its Commandant. Washington had also been a soldier and sacrificed greatly to free and unite the country.

President Lincoln had sent an envoy asking Lee to lead the Northern military and protect that unity. He was still in the Army and felt the pull of a soldier's duty to his country. What about his duty to his family and native Virginia? Should he bear arms against them? It was a dilemma of duty. This was his response to Lincoln's envoy:

> 'The future is in the hands of Providence. If the slaves of the South were mine, I would surrender them all without a struggle to avert this war.' 'Are you not sanguine of the result of this war,' queried the envoy? 'At present I am not concerned with the results,' replied Lee. 'God's will ought to be our aim, and I am contented that His designs should be accomplished and not mine.' [114]

Lee chose to resign his commission in the U.S. Army. After much anguish and prayer, he could not bring himself to raise arms against his family and native Virginia.

6

The Peacemaker

History demonstrates that it was the sovereign will of God for the nation to be united and for the blight of slavery to be removed. One can only speculate about the reasons for this. For instance, the U.S. has played a momentous role in world events since the Civil War. Could a divided nation have done so?

Regardless, the South needed a leader, and God chose Robert E. Lee. That selection cost Lee greatly. One example was the loss of beautiful Arlington. The North confiscated the plantation during the war, and, to spite Lee for taking up the Southern cause, turned the grounds into a military burial ground, Arlington National Cemetery.

Like his mother, Lee's wife Mary became an invalid, stricken with rheumatoid arthritis. She remained so for the last thirteen years of their marriage. Lee dutifully became her constant caregiver, right up to his death.

The thing that I find most noble about Robert E. Lee was how he conducted himself after the war. Two things occurred simultaneously. One, he endured much insult and injury from the government and the press. Secondly, he was enticed by numerous offers to "cash in" on his fame. Driven by duty, his response to both situations played a large part in reuniting the country, which was perilously close to falling into prolonged guerilla warfare.

Lee became a focal point of political attacks. He was charged with treason, a crime punishable by hanging. For numerous political reasons, federal prosecutors dismissed the proceedings, but President Andrew Johnson never dropped the charge. Lee responded to President Johnson's charge by applying for a pardon. This action infuriated many in the South, because it implied guilt. However, because he was so venerated, most Southern soldiers followed his lead. He had chosen to be a peacemaker.

In addition, although not bankrupt, his personal finances had been severely impacted by the war. He had lost Arlington, and he would never regain it in his lifetime. He had an invalid wife and three unmarried daughters who were dependent on him. He was tempted by numerous financial opportunities ranging from farming to business to an offer to write his memoirs of the Civil War.

Again, driven by duty, he chose to become president of a small, bankrupt university in Lexington, Virginia called Washington College. Why? Because being president of the college would allow him to influence a generation of future leaders. They would be the people who would integrate the South back into the Union.

The college offered Lee a residence with a small plot of land for growing vegetables and $1,500 in annual salary. This was money the school didn't have. In addition, he was offered a percentage of the tuition fees. The college assumed that Lee's stature would attract students, thus generating the revenue that would create his income. It was an academic version of a salesman working on commissions.

They guessed right. The next generation of leaders flocked to Lexington to study under Robert E. Lee. Lee's motive was influence, not personal gain.

After his death, Washington College was renamed Washington and Lee University. His name was now linked in an honoring and public way to the name of his hero, George Washington.

We've been to Lexington and the university many times. It's one of those places that draws us back periodically. Lee is buried next to the chapel that was the site of his funeral in 1870.

In honor of Lee, the university left his desk exactly as it was his last day there. He rose from that desk 135 years ago, went to a church meeting and then went home where he complained to his family about feeling poorly. Several days later, he died, but his powerful legacy lives on.

Lee's life continues to have influence. When we stand by his grave in Lexington, we feel his integrity. He had a significant destiny, not because he was famous or instrumental in history, but because he was obedient and responded to the appointments in his life with a sense of duty. Lee's sense of duty led to a life of self-sacrifice. A self-sacrificial life is a powerful life.

A sense of duty is a noble trait, one also manifested by Jesus. Jesus' sense of duty flowed from His love for His Heavenly Father and for mankind. Both compelled Him to spend Himself fully. The writer Anne Lamott said: "Jesus paid a debt He didn't owe because we had a debt we couldn't pay." [115]

7
Simplicity Leads to Disclosure and Intimacy with God

Beyond a sense of duty, Robert E. Lee's life message was also characterized by simplicity. By that I mean he simply responded to the events of life, his appointments, with obedience.

We can over-complicate a process that God never intended to be difficult. Not that there isn't a supernatural, mystical aspect to discovering our destinies. There surely is. But if it is really that hard, we'd never be able to find our way to a meaningful life. Lee simply responded to the situations he encountered, i.e. his appointments, with obedience and found his destiny in the process.

Understanding the mysterious aspects that made up our destinies will be part of the joy of heaven. To fully comprehend how God intricately wove together all of our appointments in life, all our experiences and relationships, into what would ultimately become our destinies will be wonderful, indeed.

Over the years, numerous Biblical truths and teachings from various Christian leaders have reinforced my belief that realizing my appointments in life is not meant to be nearly as complex as I was making it.

First, the Apostle Paul said not to be "led astray from the simplicity and purity of devotion to Christ."[116] In other words, it's a trap to over complicate things.

Oswald Chambers said: "Simplicity is the secret of seeing things clearly. Therefore, the simple thing to do is focus on our obedience to Christ." [117]

Chambers also said:

> At the beginning of the Christian life, we are full of requests of God, then we find God wants to get us into relationship with Himself, to get us in touch with His purposes…The things that make God dear to us are not so much His great big blessings as the tiny things because they show His amazing intimacy with us; He knows every detail of our individual lives. [118]

God discloses Himself to those who simply obey, and they experience intimacy with Him. That's what is evident in all the accounts of Lee's life. Jesus said that if we would keep His commands, He would disclose Himself to us (John 14:21).

Spiritually speaking, simplicity, obedience, disclosure and intimacy are linked together in a unique way. If we will simply focus on obeying God's commands, then He will disclose Himself to us, and we will experience intimacy with Him. And what would that mean? It would mean we could experience what Jesus said was the essence of eternal life (John 17:3), knowing God. The primary benefit of eternity, knowing God, can start right now, not later.

It also means by implication that life is about Him and not me and my consuming preoccupation with finding happiness. All of our appointments in life are intended to be about relating to Him. Therein we find happiness.

Finally, looking at Lee's simple obedience transports my views of destiny from one realm to another. My focus is moved from the future to the now—the current moment. It's easy to be preoccupied with the future. God uses Robert E. Lee's simple obedience to say that life is about today and how you can know God in the current moment. These moments are your appointments. Respond to them wisely, and you will find your life's message and the joy, purpose and fruitfulness you are seeking.

2

The Distinguishing Traits of God's Appointments

Appointments and Spiritual Chain Reactions: Obedience,
to Power, to Unique Character • from Chapter Seven

As we obey God, we feel the powerful effects of His truth in our lives. We become more stable and consistent in our behavior as convictions are developed, producing character. Over time these convictions cause us to live a certain way, and they become distinguishing character traits that mark our lives and impact our destinies.

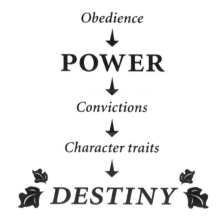

Obedience
↓
POWER
↓
Convictions
↓
Character traits
↓
DESTINY

22. God uses people and circumstances in our lives to create positive or negative models. Like General Lee, our convictions are often developed through our observations and experiences regarding these models. How have positive or negative models affected your convictions, as you applied Biblical truth to situations? Has a distinguishing character trait developed because of this?

Positive or negative models:

1. _____

_____

2. _____

_____

3. _____

_____

4. _____

_____

Applied Biblical truth:

1. _____

_____

2. _____

_____

3. _____

_____

4. _____

_____

Conviction:

1. _____

_____

2. _____

3.
_____

4.
_____

Distinguishing character trait:

1.
_____

2.
_____

3.
_____

4.
_____

23. Simplicity is the secret of seeing things clearly. It comes from focusing on obeying Christ.

If you could undo anything in your life to make it more simple, requiring obedience to Christ, what would that be?

_____

_____

_____

_____

SECTION THREE
Action Steps

There are things we can do to enhance our chances of experiencing joy, purpose and fruitfulness.

I've heard it said: "If you aim at nothing, you'll hit it." On a similar note, Yogi Berra said: "You've got to be very careful if you don't know where you're going, because you might not get there." Both statements are saying in a creative way that we need to take action. We need to be proactive, otherwise our lives can fall short, and we can compromise our destinies.

Let's look at three important action steps we can take: becoming sober-minded; living for others; and responding to our God-given boundaries.

• • • •

"So if God places me in situations of great perplexity, must He not give me much guidance; in positions of great difficulty, much grace; in circumstances of great pressure and trial, much strength?"

—Hudson Taylor
Founder, China Inland Mission

CHAPTER EIGHT
Become Sober-Minded

1
Defining Sober-Mindedness

Television personality Bryant Gumble told the story of interviewing a man who had just turned one hundred years old. Gumble asked him if he'd always aspired to live to be one hundred. The old fellow responded: "Not till I was ninety-nine."

Though humorous, the story hints at subtle truths. You could gather from his response that he's living in the moment. That's a good thing.

But what I took from the story is that it's not man's nature to consider the important realities of life, like objectively dealing with our mortality. Who wants to think about dying? It's like Woody Allen quipped: "I don't mind dying; I just don't want to be there when it happens."

When it comes to living in the moment and considering the future, the Bible appears to give contradictory instructions. It tells us to do both.

Jesus said: "So don't worry about tomorrow, for tomorrow will bring its own worries. Today's trouble is enough for today." [119] Although Jesus is talking primarily about anxiety, He also infers that we should live in the moment.

Moses said: "So teach us to number our days, that we may present to Thee a heart of wisdom." [120] In contrast to this, Moses encourages us to think strategically about our lives. We need to consider where we are in life's journey and make the best use of our time and talents. He also says to keep the end in mind for an important reason. We will have a meeting with God, and we ought to present to Him a heart of wisdom.

That has always been difficult for me to do—to live in the moment and, at the same time, think strategically about the future.

Gumble told another story that gave me a picture of this dilemma.

In an interview with a golf magazine, he described his reaction to his fiftieth birthday. He said he felt like he was "playing the fourteenth hole." I chuckled. I could relate to that since golf is a passion of mine.

By the time you get to the fourteenth hole, you sense the end is near. Most of the round is behind you, and there's only a limited amount of fun left. You're starting to get tired and concentration becomes even more important, so that you don't make mistakes due to fatigue.

Also, there's enough time left to affect your score. You can visualize the impact of a birdie or a bogey on the round. Golfers struggle to stay in the moment, just focusing on one shot at a time. Golfers, by necessity, need to practice sober-mindedness.

But what is it? Is sober-mindedness walking around with a dour expression, never smiling and always serious? Is it living like a monk, always meditating, contemplating life and never speaking?

Danish philosopher Søren Kierkegaard said: "Life is lived forward, but understood backward." [121] He's saying we should take time to study the past so we can formulate action for the future. Thinking about something in its entirety actually helps us to live more effectively in the moment.

Going back to my golf analogy, this would be like me thinking: Okay, it's the fourteenth hole. I've been out here a long time. It's natural for me to be tired. The important thing to focus on now is my posture and tempo. I've followed the instruction of both Jesus and Moses. I've taken into account the whole round of golf so that I can more effectively live in the moment. This will allow me to finish well.

The Bible, in many places, commands us to develop this trait (I Thessalonians 5:6, II Timothy 4:5, I Peter 1:13, I Peter 4:7, I Corinthians 15:34). Those verses speak to many qualities, which collectively represent sober-mindedness. It's a combination of being self-controlled, watchful, alert and sound-minded. It's an inner government of the self so that we are *pro*active in life rather than *re*active to life.

Why is sober-mindedness so important? God ministers to us in all the situations of life, during the busy hectic times, as well as the mundane. But His rich fellowship and instruction is best enjoyed in our solitude, not our busyness. Therefore, the most fundamental component of sober-mindedness is our devotional life. By this I mean our time reading, studying and meditating on scripture.

I'm also referring to our prayer life, those times when we are both talking to and listening to God, enjoying His Presence and involvement in our lives.

It's also about reading and studying anything that will help us in our quest to live a life of joy, purpose and fruitfulness. It's those disengaged times of meditation, study and prayer that give us guidance, perspective and strength. Then when we do engage in life, we are truly effective.

Jesus was the best at this. We see in His activities this pattern—engage life, then disengage. "...And vast crowds came to hear Him preach and be healed of their diseases. But Jesus often withdrew to the wilderness for prayer." [122]

Jesus gives us the fundamental reason why sober-mindedness is so important. It's recorded in Luke 19:41-44. This tells the story of His approach to Jerusalem. As He sees the city, His heart is filled with sorrow and He weeps over Jerusalem. Something happened there that deeply troubled Him. Then He describes the problem and prophesies about what will happen to Jerusalem because of its mistake—one that we do not want to make.

I especially like British translator J.B. Phillips' treatment of this passage, which follows:

And as He came nearer to the city, He caught sight of it and wept over it, saying, 'Ah, if you only knew, even at this eleventh hour, on what your peace depends—but you cannot see it. The time is coming when your enemies will encircle you with ramparts, surrounding you and hemming you in on every side. And they will hurl you and your children to the ground—yes, they will not leave you one stone standing upon another—***all because you did not recognize when God himself was visiting you!***' [123]

Approximately forty years later, in 70 A.D., that's exactly what happened. The Roman general, Titus, invaded and conquered Jerusalem, totally destroying the temple, not leaving one stone unturned.

In Jerusalem we have stood at the "Wailing Wall," the site believed to be the remaining foundation stones of Solomon's Temple, which was destroyed by the Romans. It's sobering to offer up prayers surrounded by many Jews who are truly wailing. When you consider the history and feel the political tensions between the three great religions of the world, you sense that you are standing at "ground zero" for the universe.

It was equally sobering to stand beneath the Arch of Titus in Rome. It was the Roman custom to erect monuments commemorating their military victories. Just across the street from the Coliseum, an equally sobering place, stands this incredible arch that was erected to honor the conquest and sacking of Jerusalem, something Jesus predicted roughly forty years before the actual event.

The serious mistake was that people did not recognize when God was visiting them. If we are not sober-minded, that's exactly the mistake we make. When that happens we lose the awareness of where we are in life and what we are to accomplish. We do not recognize the spiritual purpose behind the events of our lives. God's visiting us, and we just don't see it. We lose our spiritual sensitivity.

When I think about my own struggles with sober-mindedness I notice that I tend to err in two ways. First, I tend toward too much action and not enough time thinking, planning and recharging. I have some good excuses for this. The contemporary pace of life encourages this behavior. It almost demands it. Life seems to be about action and speed, not reflection. Emerging technologies facilitate the rapid pace of life. Intense competition demands it. I feel the pressure to perform, lest I fall behind. I'll go out on a limb and say this is probably true for most people. I always see people who are moving too fast, doing too much and voicing the same frustration about their pace of life.

Second, mass marketing allures me to immediate self-gratification. There is so much to do and experience. When I sense that I need a break or have some discretionary time at my disposal, there always seems to be something competing with sober-mindedness, or what

I might call strategically used time. There's a football game to watch or a round of golf to play or a movie to view or a trip to take or an item that I just must purchase. I'm inundated with things I can do that compete with a wisely used block of time.

We desperately need the nourishment that only a strong devotional life can provide. If we realized that we receive far more than we give up, then there would be no need for appeals to become sober-minded people.

A. W. Tozer said: "Back of every wasted life is a bad philosophy, an erroneous conception of life's worth and purpose." [124]

When God spoke to Elijah the prophet at Mount Horeb, He came in a gentle breeze, not in the strong wind or the earthquake or the fire (I Kings 11:13).

As I write on this cold January day, a blizzard is howling outside. The snow is swirling in the air, and the wind is rattling the windows. I've closed the drapes to help keep out the cold. A friend just called and asked for the correct time. The storm is so intense that it's left them without power for hours. Plus, her watch is broken.

I have to chuckle, because that's a good picture of what I'm trying to communicate. That's how I often feel, like I'm living in a blizzard, without any power, and not really aware what time it is in my life.

Sober-mindedness fosters spiritual sensitivity. In intimacy, God whispers to us. We must be quiet and still to hear. We must calm our spirits. In doing that, and only in doing that, will we enjoy God and receive the guidance and strength we need to appropriately engage the future, react appropriately to our appointments and have a more significant destiny.

2
Okay, but Where Do I Start?

There are two things that absolutely have to happen in order to become a sober-minded individual. Beyond that, most anything goes. But, without these two steps, nothing happens.

The first and fundamental step is to make a decision of the will to become a sober-minded individual. That leads to the second step, which is discipline. I must discipline myself and adapt my lifestyle, so I can use time wisely.

My conviction about this subject led me to an honest assessment of how I actually spent my time. Life felt busy and packed with activities. I thought I was making good use of my time and wondered how I would ever be able to carve out time for such solitude. Work couldn't go and neither could my commitment to my family.

However, as I studied my days I recognized a particular daily habit, one that had a ramification I never could have imagined. Most every night, to unwind from a typically hectic day, I would drift off to sleep watching old re-runs on television.

I got out a calculator to see how much of my life was dedicated to re-runs on an annual basis. The math went something like this, (5 nights per week x 52 weeks = 260 episodes.) That equals 130 hours a year, which I divided by 8 hours, to equate the number to an average work day. I was spending 16.25 days a year watching television!

I was genuinely shocked by that calculation. There is certainly nothing wrong with idle time. We all need some of it. But I wondered if that much time was warranted. So the question became which would be more nourishing and refreshing for my spirit and soul, television or my newfound conviction regarding sober-mindedness?

I chose to replace most of those evenings of "vegging out" on TV with reading in bed. I still watch television occasionally and enjoy it, but not as much as I've come to enjoy my reading which reinforces sober-mindedness. So I wasn't giving up a fun thing for yet another responsibility. The trade-off was really a fun thing for an even more fun thing.

We all have time available to us. We fritter away more time than we think. But most of us haven't been honest and analytical regarding how we truly spend our time.

We all have a need to relax periodically and get away from the stresses of life. But this can quickly get out of balance and that can lead us to spending this precious resource on mediocre activities. That in turn compromises our destinies.

During a recent conversation, Kathy and I were analyzing a

sensitive topic—my time on the golf course. Our conclusion had good news and bad news. The good news was that I'd played less golf during the year then we expected. The bad news was that I'd still frittered away far too much time trying to lower my handicap.

First, I tried to rationalize my behavior—well, I use the time for fellowship and building relationships with people. Those were snippets of truth, but let's face it for what it really is— addiction.

Can I really afford to do that? So one of my major goals is to limit my time on the links. Golf is great fun and, when everything else is in balance, it is truly relaxing. But it doesn't have any eternal redeeming value. In fact, it could have the opposite effect. When I spend too much time playing golf, it creates guilt, and that's never any fun.

3
The Real Issue

Our initial quest to become sober-minded people was the result of our efforts to do something very important—resolve issues in our marriage!

I take most of the blame for those problems. It was early in our marriage, and I was a confused young man. I was a "backslidden Christian" in the truest sense. My entire life was centered on my drive to be successful. This was a multi-faceted problem. First, there was the anger and guilt I felt for not being in vocational Christian work. In addition, there was fear of failure and the pressure I felt to provide for my family. Thus, I was working long hours, never available to the family and not meeting Kathy's needs.

There was also the issue of us not understanding how to relate to each other intimately. We were two naïve young people doing a poor job of communicating verbally and physically.

We reached a crisis point. We knew we had to do something, but we weren't sure what. So we decided that the first step should be to retreat from the daily grind, get away and discuss the situation.

We rented a cozy little cabin in the mountains just outside of Denver. It was wintertime, and the cabin had a wood burning fireplace.

We built fires, talked, cried, confessed things to each other, and prayed for several days as we analyzed our marriage. There were often painful interchanges accompanied by some less than gracious finger-pointing.

Thankfully, after the appropriate apologies, our retreat yielded fruit. We were able to identify areas where we could make changes and get back on track. Most of the action steps we agreed to implement had something to do with this quality of sober-mindedness.

Our crisis revealed why people aren't more sober-minded and fritter away so much precious life on frivolous things—they do not truly see their need!

The crisis showed us our need. Our emotions were numb as a result of the storm we had weathered, and we were scared because we had come close to marital disaster. We were desperate people. We were looking for a lifeline. Sober-mindedly turning to God's Word for comfort and direction was that lifeline.

In addition, I discovered that I had previously seen such pursuits as an obligation. I felt that I had to give up something that gave me pleasure to do something that was a Christian obligation. There are many appeals within Christianity to spend time in Bible study and prayer. We know we should do that. Sadly, some of the appeals come across as nagging and can produce a Christian guilt trip.

4
Practical Tips

We came away from that cabin with renewed hope and commitment. We began applying our new action steps to our lives. When I began to devote time to these activities, I was met by emotions I didn't expect. My times alone in prayer and meditation gave me more pleasure than the things I had relinquished. What I thought would be a sacrifice was not a sacrifice at all. In fact, my spirit and soul were being nourished in a way they had never been nourished before. In business we call that "trading up."

Plus, we received valuable instruction regarding God's perspective of intimacy. This came from the Bible and various Christian books on the subject. We were able to put new insights into practice, and soon we were enjoying a newfound intimacy—both verbally and physically. We began to meet each other's needs.

We also realized that our schedules were set reactively rather than proactively. We reacted to the demands and pleasures of life. Any time left over was allocated to such pursuits as prayer, reading the Bible and studying other sources that might help us mature. The problem was there was never any time left over. We decided it would be a priority to make the time available.

This brought to our attention a related problem. We seemed to be incapable of saying no to activities and commitments. Maybe it's an overused colloquialism, but it was certainly fitting. We realized that we were "jumping through a lot of other people's hoops."

So we decided to proactively block our calendars with the activities we wanted to pursue and make any competing activities, even good ones, fight to get on our calendar.

I've become quite adept at saying things like: "I'm sorry, I've got a previous commitment that night," or "I can do the meeting telephonically, but I can't be there."

In addition, we realized that we were wasting away large blocks of time in the early morning, primarily with sleep, and in the evenings with TV or movies.

We committed to doing three things; get up earlier, devote two nights a week to reading and read ourselves to sleep most nights, regardless of an evening's primary activity.

Over the years, we've come to cherish the early morning hours, even more than sleep. We feel like if we linger too long in bed, we're missing a special time with God.

We also build into our schedules regular times of disengagement. Sundays are totally off limits. That is a down day, a day of rest, reflection, and preparation for the week ahead.

Our business life had always revolved around quarters. We realized that we tended to be exhausted after three months of strenuous engagement to achieve quarterly objectives. So at the end of each quarter, we scheduled a long weekend, three or four days to go slow, analyze the past, reflect and prepare for the future.

Annually, we did much the same thing. We still do. We always take off the week between Christmas and New Year's—my favorite week of the year. That's a week of sitting in front of our fireplace focused on our devotional lives, reviewing our journals and schedules, talking and praying together.

Then we plan for the coming year. I especially like to delve into my schedule books and compare the current year to past years. It gives us a good overall view of whether we are making any progress regarding the use of our time as we try to accomplish our goals. That week is a thoroughly slow and contemplative time.

I mentioned earlier that two imperative things have to happen. We have to willfully commit ourselves to becoming sober-minded people and we need to follow up the commitment with discipline. There's no right way for the discipline to manifest itself. Anything goes. There is no one right way to become sober-minded. We have the pleasure of creating a system that's right for us. All the key elements will be there, but we can do them in different ways.

I'll describe the fundamental system that has evolved for us. Hopefully, this will serve as a stimulus and provide ideas for your own approach.

5
The Word, Meditation, and Prayer

This is the most important and fundamental part of any system for becoming a balanced, sober-minded individual. God directs our destinies, and we must be able to hear His voice. It is through our devotional lives that He reveals our appointments, giving us the understanding we need to respond appropriately to the circumstances before us.

We should approach our time in scripture and prayer with an attitude of spiritual formation, not information gathering. The attitude ought to be one of applying what I encounter in scripture to my life. It's as if the passages are personal letters to us from a loving parent giving us encouragement and guidance for life.

Growing spiritually is like laying railroad track (see illustration below). The two rails are nailed to the ties which are firmly placed on the railroad bed. This provides stability and direction, so trains can proceed from one point to another, eventually reaching their destinations.

SPIRITUAL
GROWTH

PRAYER

MEDITATION

PRAYER

MEDITATION

Scriptural Truth　　　　　*Action Taken*

Similarly, we have a destination we want to reach—spiritual maturity, or Christ likeness. The left rail represents scriptural truth. The right rail represents action to be taken. In our analogy, the ties represent meditation and prayer. We think, study and pray over scriptural truth with an attitude of applying that scriptural truth to our life. We are laying track, or creating spiritual formation, which leads us to our spiritual destination. This is how we grow spiritually.

This process happens in one of two ways. We might be meditating on a passage of scripture, and the Holy Spirit brings to mind a situation in our life where we need to apply the scriptural truth. Or we might be thinking about a situation and turn to the Bible, allowing the Holy Spirit to lead us to the appropriate passages to contemplate and apply to the situation before us.

Here's an example of laying spiritual railroad track. Once I had a strong difference of opinion with a beloved family member. I was angry but also concerned about protecting the relationship. I used my primary reference tools, which for me are a Bible dictionary and a concordance, to find verses in the Bible dealing with anger.

I also prayed because I knew I'd need help with my attitude. My fundamental instinct was to strike back and defend myself, which I already knew was an inappropriate response. The real issue was how to maintain a clear conscience before God with my actions, not how to win a family dispute.

That allowed me to approach my analysis with an attitude of application, putting into action whatever I might find. My study led me to Ephesians 4:29:

> Let no unwholesome word proceed from your mouth, but only such a word as is good for edification according to the need of the moment, that it may give grace to those who hear. [125]

That verse summed everything up quite nicely. It gave me the action to be taken and showed me what conduct would be pleasing to God. However, I still needed the strength to actually put the verse into practice. That required more prayer.

I'm happy to say that the confrontation had a positive outcome. The gentle and kind approach was totally disarming, allowing us to quickly move the conversation toward our love for each other. Disaster was averted, and I was thankful that God had led me through it, giving me the insight and strength to respond to an appointment appropriately.

I reiterate that the key to a healthy devotional life is to have an attitude of application. Have questions in mind. Perhaps you might ask yourself if there is a command to obey, a sin to avoid or a habit to cultivate.

Prayer should be thought of as a two-way dialogue between us and God. We talk, then pause and listen. It's not a one-way monologue of request. I often put my name into the text I am reading and then pray it back to God. Then I sit quietly and listen, thinking about how the text could be applied to my life. That application is in effect God's answer.

Here's a small example of how that looks. I'll personalize Psalms 16:7-8. I pray: "I will bless the Lord who guides Bill Williams, even at night my heart instructs me. I know the Lord is always with Bill Williams. I will not be shaken, for the Lord is right beside Bill Williams."

Then as I am still and listen, the Spirit of God within me prompts me to consider that my every thought, even as I lay in bed at night, should be focused on Christ and ready to receive instruction (verse seven). Because God is totally faithful, I can, as an act of the will, not be alarmed with bad news, because He will be there to support me (verse eight).

These observations represent only some fundamentals to keep in mind regarding a healthy devotional life. There is much to be said and, thankfully, there are plenty of good books available on the subject. A personal favorite that I would recommend is *Savoring God's Word*, by Jan Johnson, published by NavPress.

6

Pilgrimages

In addition to cultivating good devotional habits, there are other things we can do to be sober, alert people, in synch with God's purposes for our lives. Here are a few of our favorites.

We enjoy vacationing with purpose and have been blessed with the resources to travel. So we take what we call destiny pilgrimages. We go places where we can immerse our self in an event or someone's life. The experiences always provide snippets of wisdom we can apply to our own life and cause us to reflect on our mortality.

More importantly, pilgrimages give us a renewed sense of conviction about the gravity, value and importance of life. We come away with a rekindled commitment to understand and meet our appointments in a manner that will please God.

We've sat at the summit of Little Round Top at Gettysburg and considered what happened there. We've stood in the amphitheater at

Ephesus where Paul preached and wandered the halls of Westminster Abby in London where so many historical figures are interred. Such experiences have a penetrating effect and move us to self-examination.

Monticello, the home of Thomas Jefferson, has a particularly unique effect on us. We've made many pilgrimages there. There's just something about Monticello that helps us capture the rhythm and season of our life together. For some mysterious reason, Monticello always leaves us with a renewed sense of purpose and direction.

7
Journals

Journaling represents a major component of our system to foster sober-mindedness. I've learned that I cannot write as fast as I can think, so writing has the effect of slowing me down.

It's funny to look at my journal entries. In each one, my writing is almost illegible in the beginning. Then as I start to unwind it becomes readable.

I use a specific trick to keep myself writing. I have to go to New York City often for business. There's an elegant store in Mid-Town Manhattan that carries beautiful leather writing journals from an English company. These journals are outrageously expensive. I buy one for Kathy and me every year. I feel so convicted about the price that it motivates me to make sure I use it. I realize that's fairly perverse logic, but it helps foster the writing habit.

There are many reasons why I love journaling. One has to do with something I heard Chuck Swindoll, the renowned pastor, writer and speaker, say at a conference. He mentioned that after his father died, he found his dad's writing particularly comforting and instructive, almost a way of extending the relationship. I want this to be true for my boys as well. I write primarily to enhance my relationship with Christ, but also to capture truths that might help guide the boys after I'm gone. Within its pages they will find my heart, my joys, my disappointments, my victories and defeats. Perhaps it will be comforting to them.

Our journals are literally the command center for our spiritual

pilgrimages. We write about our activities, our feelings and our observations from life. We also record insights from scripture and write
down many of our prayers. We especially note if a prayer has been
answered. They are literally the account of God's dealings with us
over the years.

8

Chronological Timelines

The idea here is to get your life on paper in a linear fashion for
the purpose of analysis. Please refer to the example in the workbook.
We do this by drawing vertical columns on paper, each column rep-
resenting a year. At the top of the column we write the year and our
ages. Then between the columns we record a number of significant
things pertinent to the year. We note key people we've met, where
we worked and lived, a move or career change, if any. We also note
any other event that was important that year including such things
as successes, failures and things we felt compelled to do. Then horizontally, to the left of the columns, we write down the conclusions
to our analysis.

This linear approach to viewing your life enhances perspective
and creates vision. It provides a view of life over longer periods of
time, thereby demonstrating progress and purpose. It's encouraging.

Let me illustrate. I mentioned earlier that I had, in effect, two
careers—one in healthcare and the other as a vocational Christian
worker. Then I talked about the illuminating and somewhat mysterious promise of revelation from Isaiah 61 that links these two worlds
together for me.

The chronological timeline reinforced that leading by pointing
out, on one page, several important occurrences. The most fundamental observation was that we'd come into contact with significant
leaders from both spheres of influence. God gave us mentors from
both worlds. We concluded that those two spheres of influence were
intended to be where our life's work would occur. We also concluded
that the focus of our calling would be an effort to integrate those two
diverse worlds together in a unique way.

As we moved between the two worlds, we could clearly see a process at work either drawing us into or sending us out of one of those spheres of influence. But it was a process we weren't controlling. God was. As we looked at the progression, year by year, we could clearly see purpose, direction and God's intervention.

The timeline also compliments and reinforces other parts of our approach to foster sober-mindedness. For instance, our studies of the Bible and history demonstrated three primary seasons of life for many people. First there is an early season of training and preparation. Then there is a second season where the core of one's life work is actually executed. Then there's a later stage of mentorship, influencing future generations as they progress through the first two stages.

This cycle is a generalization and might not hold true for all people. But it is a prevalent pattern in both the Bible and history. It certainly is true for us.

Again, Robert E. Lee's life is a good example. First, there were the early years of preparation. Those years gave him the training and growth in character that he would need for the tough years before him. Next was his most strategic appointment, leading the Army of Northern Virginia for five years. Lastly, as President of Washington College, he mentored the future generation of leaders for the South. This season also lasted five years, the final five of his life.

As we looked back over our shoulders at the early years, we couldn't help but laugh at ourselves. Those had been frustrating years, but the timeline ultimately called attention to training being accomplished, training that we did not recognize. It also called attention to a lack of patience on our part. We had plans and God had plans, but His played out a lot slower than ours.

9
Scripture Memory

It's impossible to be around The Navigators and not get indoctrinated with the importance of scripture memory. It's certainly a discipline but can make an invaluable contribution to sober-mindedness.

Although it can be hard to get started, afterwards scripture memory can become addictive. I say this because of the benefits that it generates. Storing God's truth in our minds provides a valuable tool to the Holy Spirit for communication. He brings those truths to mind to convict and guide us on a moment-by-moment basis as we encounter our appointments in life. We are literally dialoguing with God, utilizing His Word.

I recall a time when we were on Navstaff. I was having a nice afternoon and quite unexpectedly received a phone call from my college wrestling coach. We hadn't talked in years, so I knew something was wrong.

He proceeded to tell me a gruesome story. One of my ex-teammates had a brain tumor, and the surgery to remove the tumor had complications. During the operation several nerves were destroyed, and others were traumatized. This left my friend partially paralyzed on the left side of his body.

I was stunned. At one time we had been good friends. In addition to the wrestling team, we had also played on the University rugby team, been fraternity brothers and worked the same summer job for several years.

I needed to get away and think about the news, so I slipped into my jogging clothes and took a long run. My mind was filled with many thoughts. I pictured this once gifted athlete now crippled for life. I thought about his family. His wife was a fine woman. With three kids, she was surely overwhelmed.

Then, from out of nowhere, a memory verse flashed across my mind: "Do not withhold good from those to whom it is due when it is in your power to do it." [126] It's as if God said: "What's stopping you from going there and helping? You can make the time, and Kathy can handle the kids."

We later decided that's what I needed to do. The visit helped their family during a rough time, but, in reality, it did far more for me. I assisted with the kids, cleaned their house, nursed my friend and worked with him during his grueling physical therapy sessions. I left about a week later, deeply affected by the experience. That was a personal appointment for me and was delivered to me by the Holy Spirit using His Word implanted in my mind.

It seems to me that the pressures of life often lie to us, telling us that our worst fears will come to pass. We need to be reassured that the lies are just that—lies. Only God's Word is truth.

Scripture memory provides that stabilizing, calming effect I often need. During difficult times, it's reassuring to meditate on various passages. They diffuse anxiety and reset a correct perspective. Again there are no rules regarding scripture memory. Just pick a time and place that's right for you. It's more a matter of resolution.

The great Civil War leader and deeply committed Christian, General "Stonewall" Jackson, wrote in a book he called his "Personal Code of Conduct" the following: "You may be whatever you resolve to be." [127] That strikes at the heart of the issue.

Gordon MacDonald, author of *Ordering Your Private World*, articulated the issue in this way: "If my private world is in order, it will be because I have made a daily determination to see time as God's gift and worthy of careful investment." [128]

We need to let God's truth swirl around in our heads and lead our thoughts in a spiritual direction. Then we will know what time it is in our lives, recognize the spiritual significance of our *appointments* and respond appropriately to them. Then we will experience more joy, purpose and fruitfulness.

3
Action Steps

Become Sober-Minded • from Chapter Eight

Developing sober-mindedness is crucial, because God speaks to us in the solitude of our devotional lives. It is important to not only live in the moment, but also to think strategically about the future. As was discussed in this chapter, we need to consider where we are in life and make the best use of our time and talents, because we will have a meeting with God in the end.

24. The most fundamental component of sober-mindedness is our devotional life—our time reading, studying and meditating on scripture. We need to allow God to speak to us, so we can apply His truth to our lives. Using the "Railroad Track Illustration," fill in the spaces below.

List some verses of scripture that have stood out in your devotional times, their personal meanings to you and the actions they have inspired:

Scriptural Truth:

1. _____

_____

_____

2. _____

_____

_____

Meditation and Prayer:

1. _____

_____

2. _____

_____

Action Taken:

1. _____

_____

2. _____

_____

List some situations that have demanded your response, the scriptural truth (or verse) you found to help, the key result of meditating and praying about this verse, and the action you took or will take:

Situation:

1. _____

_____

2. _____

_____

Scriptural Truth:

1. _____

_____

2. _____

_____

Meditation and Prayer:

1. _____

_____

2. _____

_____

Action Taken:

1. _____

_____

2. _____

_____

25. Among other scripture references, I Thessalonians 5:16 tells us: "So then let us not sleep as others do, but let us be alert and sober." There is value in contemplative thought and analysis. In reflecting on the past, it is possible for us to formulate actions for the future by seeing patterns and how significant events and people have shaped our path. Use the chart on the next page to create your own chronological timeline. You may add pages as necessary. Decide on the years of your life that you wish to analyze, then enter the year at the top of each column. Within each column, keep track of key people you met; key life events such as career changes, moves, births, deaths, accidents, successes, and failures; ages; key impressions about the year; and things you felt compelled to do. Blank spaces are included so you may add another category if you wish.

YEAR	
KEY PEOPLE MET	
KEY EVENTS • *Career Changes* • *Moves* • *Births/Deaths* • *Success/Failures*	
AGE • *Yourself* • *Spouse* • *Children*	
KEY IMPRESSIONS	
WHAT WAS I COMPELLED TO DO?	

26. In creating a system that's right for you, several other ideas were presented: spending time reading the Word, meditating on scripture, prayer, taking pilgrimages, keeping journals and scripture memory.

I feel I'm lacking the following in my approach to sober-mindedness, and here is what I intend to do to change this:

_____

_____

_____

_____

_____

_____

_____

_____

_____

_____

_____

_____

_____

_____

_____

_____

_____

CHAPTER NINE
Live for People

1
The Worth of the Individual

One of my major appointments in life spanned from 1988 to 2000. In 1988, I became the second employee of the Pyxis Corporation, located in San Diego, California. It was a fledgling start-up company founded to automate drug delivery in hospitals. The first year there were just a few of us working in an office no bigger than a bedroom. But by the mid-1990s, there were two thousand employees, and the company was generating several hundred million dollars in annual revenue.

In the early nineties, Pyxis was a "darling of Wall Street," having been a spectacular IPO that experienced a meteoric rise in stock price. Needless to say, investors loved it.

However, in the mid-nineties the company staggered. It wasn't much, but it doesn't take much bad news to create a negative impact on stock. Consequently, an S&P 500 company purchased the company for nearly a billion dollars. That's a big number, but it represented only two-thirds of the market valuation the company had once enjoyed.

At the time of the acquisition, the company was struggling. Its numbers were falling. It was late in releasing its next generation technology that would put the company back on track. There were numerous cultural issues between the two diverse companies, and many of the best people had either retired or accepted positions with other companies.

We were among those who had retired. I say we, because my whole family had been employed there. Kathy had worked in administration, and our two sons had worked in manufacturing, earning a few extra dollars after school and in the summers. We moved back from San Diego to our beloved Colorado and built our home. We'd always wanted to write this book and had started that endeavor.

Going to Pyxis had been about fulfilling the central part of my calling to integrate my faith into my business world—to attempt to blend my two diverse spheres of influence into one. In my mind, I was doing this with God and for God, not for myself.

Although a great blessing, my years at Pyxis were filled with pressure, tense conflict resolution, responsibility and exhausting travel. I was tired. I had gone to Pyxis intent on fully spending myself, and I did. I had learned from wrestling in my youth, and I wasn't going to look over my shoulder after this business experience, wondering if I'd given it my best.

But God had yet another appointment in mind for me at Pyxis. Soon after the acquisition the Chairman and CEO of the acquiring company asked me to come back as President and integrate Pyxis into the new organization.

The magnitude of the company's prior success made me feel pressure and forlornness with that appointment. I was concerned that I wouldn't have the emotional and physical energy to see the appointment through. Plus, I understood the problems and issues at Pyxis and was glad I wasn't going to be the one responsible for fixing them, or so I thought. I felt it was time for the next generation of leaders, people who were younger, smarter and less tired to take the baton and run with it.

The appointment materialized quickly and left me feeling powerless and discouraged for several years. But it taught me much about the subject of this chapter—the worth of the individual and the importance of living for people.

2
Chariots of Fire

Here's how the appointment came into being. After the acquisition, I was asked to make several trips around the country to encourage the employees and hopefully dispel their fears and concerns regarding the coming changes. During one of those trips, I received a call from the Chairman and CEO of the acquiring company asking to get together to talk about the recent acquisition. Coincidently, I was going to be in his city later that week, so we arranged a meeting.

I've come to call such coincidences "God things." Actually, I don't believe they are coincidences at all. They are divine *appointments*. This one certainly was.

I was in Chicago when I received the call. I spoke to the employees in the morning. In the afternoon, I accompanied them to the opening home game for the Chicago Cubs.

It was a beautiful, warm April day at Wrigley Field. From the charged atmosphere, I sensed that it was a rite of passage for the Chicagoans from a gloomy winter to the greatly anticipated joys of spring.

It was a typical baseball setting. It was between innings as I watched the grounds crew groom the field. The people around me talked, laughed, munched on hot dogs, ate peanuts and sipped beer. Usually, organ music blared from the stadium speakers but not that day

Suddenly, the stadium was filled with the beautiful theme song from the movie *Chariots of Fire*, and a chill ran down my spine. A sobering realization raced through my head. I intuitively sensed that it was just a matter of time before my retirement would come to a screeching halt.

Kathy and I have an unusual and poignant relationship with that song. God's leading can come in many creative ways, and that song has been an instrument He's used to lead and encourage us over the years.

It all started back when we were deciding to leave The Navigator staff and return to business. The Academy Award-winning movie had just come out, and we were much moved by how Eric Liddell lived by his faith in the real world. This was no "closet Christian." We were convicted that we needed to do exactly the same thing, only in the context of the business community. He became a model for us. We read about his life and watched the movie many times.

Then we made the switch, and within a few years I began working for Pyxis as its first VP of Marketing and Sales. But the goal was not about business success. The goal was to use our time at Pyxis as a ministry, a calling, and to have the same attitude toward business that Liddell had toward amateur athletics.

From 1983 to 1999, God used that song many times to both lead and bolster our spirits. We never told anyone about those times but cherished them in our hearts. I have recorded thirty-one entries in my journal where we coincidentally or, better yet, miraculously heard that song. The song would come to us in airports, hotels, stores and taxi cabs.

And it would come at exactly the right times, more often than not moving us to tears. We were always amazed at how God was so in tune with our emotional state. He saw our discouragement and always knew when we were on the brink of giving up. It was as if He were saying: "Keep on. Don't quit."

This happened in bizarre places, both in this country and internationally. Once while deeply discouraged and exhausted from business travel, the song came to me on a rental car bus leaving the airport in Glasgow, Scotland. Once we were in Athens, Greece, the song found us in a far away hotel, as we were struggling with important issues. The song hadn't been popular for years, and it's not exactly a staple in the Greek musical culture.

My journal reveals that it had been over a year since we'd had an experience with *Chariots of Fire*. However, it loudly filled Wrigley Field on that beautiful April day in 1996. It was an important *appointment* for me, and I always felt like God wanted to make absolutely sure I got the message.

I sensed that it was just a matter of time until the Chairman and CEO would ask me to return and be President of Pyxis. It would be an honor but one I wasn't seeking. I thought about the company's issues and its recent performance. I also thought about the expectations that would be placed on me. I immediately felt the weight and burden of leadership. For a brief season I had a reprieve from that feeling, and it felt good. Now it would return, and there would be more responsibility than ever. This time *Chariots* was a charge to action.

However, as I sat in the stands and meditated on this possibility, I thought of Romans 8:28. I realized that God does cause all things to work together for good. Things would happen that would eventually prove good for me, even if they were painful.

I looked around at many of my friends and fellow workers. I had to admit I cared about the company and its employees. If I could make a contribution at a tough time in the company's evolution, then I needed to do so. Maybe I wasn't as tired as I thought. Evidently, God didn't think so. Even if I was, God could give me the strength to see this thing through.

Then about a month later, my intuition became reality. I became President of Pyxis Corporation. So with a sense of reluctance and foreboding, I manned my post.

I'll never forget a day shortly after my *appointment* was announced. The Chairman was a fine man, a man I respected. But he was as intense a businessman as I'd ever met. He walked up to me at a company meeting, touched his finger to my sternum and said: "I paid a billion dollars for this company. I expect you to turn it into three billion!"

3
Forget the Honeymoon

That sets the stage for the great lesson I learned about the worth of the individual and the need for us to live for people, if we really want a significant destiny.

For the next two-and-a-half years, we labored to get the company healthy again. It was just as painful as I expected. During those years, we were at our home in Colorado maybe three or four days a month. Some months, we weren't able to get back at all. This left us feeling homesick and a little disoriented. We were nomads with no sense of permanent community.

In the process, we had to reorganize the company. This meant firing people and eliminating some positions, which always creates political tension in a company. This is a time invariably characterized by dealing with litigation and averting possible litigation.

People I had originally recruited to Pyxis and counted on to help right the ship were leaving. Although it wasn't right to harbor such feelings, I couldn't help but feel personally abandoned when they left the company.

Significantly, there was the issue of the company's weak performance. We were part of a publicly traded company, and we were not meeting investor expectations. Rightly so, it was my job to take the full brunt of the criticism, which was painful and humiliating. Even though I was the President, I felt powerless to effect change quickly enough.

Far and away, the company's biggest need was to release the next version of its software, which was named *2000 RX*. Frustrated customers needed to upgrade to this more feature-rich and robust system. Potential new customers were holding off purchases, while they waited for the new release.

Unfortunately, the process was time consuming. First, cross-functional teams, mainly from marketing and research and development, had to design the software. Then, R&D had to write the code. Then, the software went to the quality assurance department to be tested before release.

We had several problems. First our cross-functional teams were acting more like dysfunctional teams. We fixed that. But we had a void of leadership in R&D, as we were searching for a new Vice President for the department.

I tried to fill the void by chairing the staff meetings in the meantime. This was a joke because I have as much technical capability as a rock. I understood about every third word of what was being said.

In spite of this, those meetings are a fond memory for me because of the people. I enjoyed the engineers, especially their honesty and candor. There wasn't a political bias in any of them. If you wanted to know how things were really going in the company, just ask them. They were more than happy to tell you. However, they were gracious, and we developed a sense of camaraderie. In reality, they probably just felt sorry for me. Regardless, we were able to establish a sense of urgency and accountability around getting the software written.

4
God Bless Jorge

The software eventually got written and was given to the Quality Assurance Department (Q.A.) for testing. The really important step, though, was to get it out into our Beta site accounts for field-testing. There's nothing like the real world. Some things simply can't be simulated in a lab.

That's where a fine, soft-spoken and extremely conscientious young man named Jorge comes into the story. At the time, he was the most important man in the company. Jorge was the Q.A. engineer responsible for working with the customers in our seven Beta sites, installing and field-testing the software.

Jorge was working at a grueling pace. Then something terrible happened. He had left one of our Beta sites in the Midwest and was heading to the Kansas City airport. The weather was bad, and he lost control of his vehicle, resulting in an accident. Luckily, an ambulance was right behind him and was able to rush him to the University of Kansas Medical Center. The fast response time saved his life.

But Jorge was badly injured. He ended up being hospitalized at the K.U. Medical Center for months and underwent numerous surgeries, one of which was a leg amputation. Needless to say, his life and his family members' lives were in disarray. They were devastated. His forthcoming marriage plans were disrupted. His family had to live in a strange city and visit the hospital daily for months. A few months later, Jorge got to return home to San Diego.

The accident brought our Beta site activity to an instant halt. But Jorge was a much respected employee and his colleagues in Q.A. adjusted and filled the void, eventually getting the work done.

Finally, after two very painful years, the company became healthy again. It was exceeding its financial projections, releasing new technology and fully integrated into its parent company.

I could take absolutely no credit for this turnaround. The success belonged to committed, talented, hardworking people within the organization, conscientiously doing their jobs. They were the most important people in the company. Although the ultimate responsibility was mine, I was totally dependent on the employees to stabilize the company.

At that time we held a national meeting for all our employees. Part of my job was to deliver the keynote message, defining who we were as a company and speaking to our direction for the future—a business version of the State of the Union address.

I took this responsibility especially seriously. I knew my commitment was coming to an end. I was more than exhausted, but I felt the job had been accomplished. I could go back to the parent company and say with a clear conscience that the company was in good shape.

We had fought many battles together as a team. I was extremely indebted to the employees and felt much attached to them. I wanted that speech to be a way of saying goodbye and to thank them in a way that honored employees and, at the same time, charted the course for the future.

I spent much time pondering all that had happened and questioned what led to the company's success. I drew two conclusions. It was due to the incredible worth of individuals and the importance of living for people.

That's why Pyxis had reclaimed its success. It was a company full of individuals who were worthy, endowed by God with various talents. They recognized the importance of their work, and regardless of titles or ego, banded together and used their respective talents for the common good.

It seemed to me that there was not a more appropriate example of those truths than Jorge. He represented what was the "Pyxis spirit." He was a talented engineer who worked diligently for the good of others. The work he started led to the company's ultimate success.

So I gave the speech and looked fondly down at Jorge. He was sitting in his wheelchair, next to his fiancé and his colleagues from Q.A. It was a delight for me to honor this man who had been through so much adversity.

However, before I could really finish talking, the employees rose to their feet to give Jorge a huge ovation. There were over two thousand people in that ballroom, and there was hardly a dry eye in the place.

I was very much moved by this experience. I fully realized how utterly dependent I was on the goodwill and efforts of those people. I owed them so much.

5

Significant Destinies Are Available to Everyone

Unfortunately, those at the top receive an undue amount of the credit for successful ventures. It was certainly so with Pyxis. I'm sure that I received more recognition than Jorge.

But God will not be mocked. He knows those who truly did the work and what their motives were. One day each person's rightful praise will come to them from the Just and Righteous Judge.

The late Mother Teresa said: "None of us can do great things, but we can do small things with great love." [129]

Therefore, we can live significant lives as lay people. I'd like to re-emphasize that destiny is not something reserved for the elite and famous in society. That is a misconception. It's for everyone. Regardless of your role in life, you are important. You have value and the potential to do great things. When I say great, I do not mean at all something that will bring you worldly recognition. I mean something that will please God and result in eternal reward.

It's easy to measure significance by wrong values. The world ascribes value to such things as fame, success and position. These things are external, visible, measurable and temporal—their reward is realized on this side of the grave.

However, God determines the true standards of greatness, and His values are exactly the opposite of the world system. He searches our motives and watches to see if we will embrace His values by living a life of selflessness, love and servanthood. Anyone is capable of doing those things in virtually any sphere of life.

The motives that stimulate our actions are internal, invisible and incapable of being measured by man. One day in eternity, God will reward motives that were righteous and godly.

I remember a situation a few years ago that demonstrated how this misconception about significance and greatness could rob a person of joy, purpose and fruitfulness.

I had been asked to speak at a conference in Dallas, Texas. As I do in any talk, I wove in comments regarding this misconception.

Afterwards, a woman and her husband approached me. She was in tears and had obviously been touched by something I said. She then told me about the guilt she felt because of a perceived lack of purpose in her life.

She was a homemaker and a substitute grade school teacher. Her husband had a position in the community that afforded him much recognition. She constantly compared herself to her husband and, consequently, came to believe a lie that what she did wasn't as important. That lie cost her much happiness. I don't know why or how, but God used my comments to clarify her thinking and release her from the guilt.

I saw her about three months later. I was back in Texas doing some follow up work with the organization that sponsored the speaking event. She was beaming and anxious to tell me a story. She proceeded to tell me how things had gone after the conference. She was no longer comparing herself to her husband. She had a sense of calling which, in turn, purified her motives about her service in her home and school.

Then one day, literally over the backyard fence, one of her neighbors commented on her noticeable change in demeanor. This provided a chance for the woman to tell her neighbor about what had occurred in her life. That struck a nerve with the neighbor. This in turn led to a deeper friendship and a chance for the school teacher/mom to influence the life of the other woman in a positive spiritual way.

It was pleasing to observe this process and to see the woman clearly recognizing the importance of her appointments. She was not living under the cloud of a lie and was experiencing joy, purpose and fruitfulness. It was obvious that she was pleasing God and enjoying every minute of it.

6
We Are Eternal

The Bible says that only two things endure throughout eternity—the Word of God and people.

Isaiah the prophet rightly prophesied: "The grass withers, and the flowers fade, but the Word of our God stands forever." [130]

Then Jesus soberly proclaimed: "...I assure you, when you refused to help the least of these my brothers and sisters, you were refusing to help Me. And they will go away into eternal punishment, but the righteous will go into eternal life." [131]

I've talked to many people over the years about Christianity. I'm always amazed how some people don't believe those two truths. They assume their non-belief renders them untrue. The statements are true anyway. Prior to Christopher Columbus, people believed the world was flat. That belief didn't make it so. The world was round anyway.

Likewise, people will live forever. Atheistic or agnostic beliefs do not alter this truth. Creation, as we know it, will not last forever, nor will nations nor success nor anything material.

Is there anything in life that God values more than people? Oswald Chambers said: "To be a disciple means to deliberately involve yourself in God's interest in other people." [132]

And where are those people located? They are scattered throughout virtually every sphere of society. That's where lay Christians also happen to be, strategically dispersed throughout society. Therefore, we are presented with an incredible opportunity to influence people with the love of Jesus Christ.

However, it's easy to assume that some spheres of influence are more important than others. They are not.

I saw a beautiful picture of this truth once in Baltimore, Maryland. In the process, I learned much from two simple yet profound men who understood the worth of the individual and the importance of living to serve people.

I was on a business trip and enjoying a lunch break as I wandered through a shopping area in Baltimore's Inner Harbor. I noticed a crowd that had gathered by a shoeshine stand. As I approached, I heard the rhythmic jingle of bells interspersed with the popping sounds of shoe shining cloths.

The man making all the noise was no ordinary man. He was nicknamed "Jingles," and he was giving a unique performance. He had little bells attached to his wrists and was dancing and humming as he shined shoes. His shoeshine cloth cracked loudly and crisply to the beat of the song he was humming.

It was a unique sight, watching Jingles lift people's spirits and bring gaiety into their otherwise drab business day. People were laughing and clapping to his beat.

It was entertaining to watch, but it fascinated me on a deeper level. Here was a man affecting people. It was more than entertainment or a shoeshine. It was an optimistic statement about excellence and pride in one's work. It was a sermon on accepting who you are, feeling good about it and then using those God-given attributes to touch those around you.

On the walls behind Jingle's stand were newspaper clippings about him and pictures of famous people whose shoes he'd shined. There were pictures of him on a popular morning television show. I've never been interviewed by *The Today Show* or *Good Morning America,* but Jingles had.

I left marveling at how God can use very simple things to teach profound truths. I was challenged to reevaluate my attitude toward my own work. I wasn't as optimistic about my work as Jingles was his.

But the lesson didn't end there. I was back in Baltimore a few months later and made it a point to stop by the Inner Harbor area to watch Jingles again. As before, his shoeshine stand was congested with people. It was the kind of congestion you experience at an airport when everyone is trying to get on the plane at the same time. I angled through the crowd trying to get a view and was surprised by what I saw.

Jingles wasn't there. Instead, I saw a young man giving much the same type of performance. One of my fellow spectators told me it was Jingles' son.

That sparked my curiosity and made me think about my relationship to my sons. After a while, the young man decided to take a lunch break. The crowd began to disperse, giving me an opportunity to introduce myself and ask him a few questions.

First, I asked him why he was shining shoes. He said it was because he wanted to be like his dad. Then I asked if he would take over the business when his father retired. He responded: "Dad will never retire. He loves what he does too much. He'd miss all the people."

His comments were very honoring to his father. It was obvious this young man loved and respected his father. To him, shining shoes was a noble calling. Jingles was leaving a legacy to the world in the person of his son.

This time, I left the Inner Harbor feeling deeply convicted about how I was doing as a father. Would my sons ever feel that way about me?

People are the most important thing in life, regardless of their sphere of influence. What we do will affect those around us. A lay Christian's influence can yield one of three results. Our lives will draw people closer to Jesus Christ, drive them further away or, because of our indifference, leave no impact at all. Obviously, two of those results are not good.

God has a plan, and lay people are part of it. If we strive to live for people, trying to reflect Jesus back to those in our spheres of influence, we will make a positive contribution to His Kingdom. We will view our appointments appropriately. We will move toward a more significant destiny. And we will experience more joy, purpose and fruitfulness in our lives.

For David, after he served the purpose of God in his own generation, fell asleep, and was laid among his fathers.... [133]

7
The Most Influential People in Your Life

Once, while discussing the worth of the individual, Kathy and I decided to make a list of the people who had influenced us most in life. We made a small list, identifying only four people. We were amazed at who we chose. Over the years, we've done this same exercise with many people. Asking someone about the most influential people in their life makes stimulating dinner conversation. People's answers are always interesting and seem to reflect the same distinction as ours; they almost always say that those who influenced them the most were obscure by the world's standards.

I can't recall anyone ever telling us they were deeply influenced by a famous person. They tend to be those closest to us: a family member, a teacher, a neighbor, a friend or an employer.

Here's a snapshot of my list with a brief statement as to why the person was so influential in my life:

1. **My grandmother.** *She planted the spiritual seeds in my life.*

2. **My father.** *He showed me what fatherhood and integrity in business was all about. His was a model worthy of emulation.*

3. **My grade school principal.** *He was the best example of excellence in leadership I've ever seen. This man handled authority wisely.*

4. **My third grade teacher.** *She created a love for reading and learning that remains a driving force in my life.*

These people had something in common. They all lived in relative obscurity. They were not rich, nor famous, nor historically relevant individuals. However, they were important people to me, and I'm grateful my life came into contact with theirs.

Everyone wields influence. The question is: will that influence be spiritually positive, spiritually negative or spiritually indifferent?

8
Concluding Thoughts

Thus far in this section, we have discussed two action steps that help us recognize God's purpose for our lives. First, we must develop the quality of sober-mindedness. We must periodically disengage from life for the purpose of prayer, meditation and study. This enables us to engage life with purpose.

Secondly, we have noted the worth of the individual. We should live loving and serving others, not ourselves. Life is about giving, not taking.

Now we turn our attention to the third thing we need to do—respond appropriately to the boundaries in our lives. Perhaps nothing in life has the capacity to create more joy, or wreak more havoc, than how we react to the boundaries that are imposed upon us.

3
Action Steps

Live for People • from Chapter Nine

God has a plan and lay people are a part of it. If we strive to live for people, trying to reflect Jesus back to those in our spheres of influence, we will make a positive contribution to His plan.

27. Here is a list of the four most influential people in my life and how they affected me:

1. _____

_____

_____

2. _____

_____

_____

3. _____

_____

_____

4. _____

_____

_____

CHAPTER TEN
Responding to the Boundaries of Life

1
Glenwood Canyon

King David said: "The lines have fallen to me in pleasant places; indeed my heritage is beautiful to me." [134] David truly loved Israel, but a study of this text in Hebrew reveals that he was referring to more than his love for Israel.

He was inferring that he was content with the major circumstances of his life, and Israel was the beloved setting where those circumstances occurred. He saw this as a gift from God. He was thankful to God for many things: the moment in time in which he lived, where he lived, what he had been called to do and his talents and abilities. Those things were all boundaries, God-ordained boundaries, and David trusted God that they were right for him. He rested in that trust and enjoyed pleasant fellowship with God.

God uses boundaries in a mysterious and wonderful way. They provide structure, meaning, clarity, identity and beauty to life. Our home state of Colorado serves as a geographic example of those truths. We feel the same way about Colorado as I'm sure David felt about Israel. What a privilege it is to live amidst the grandeur and majesty of the Rocky Mountains.

There is a particularly beautiful place close to our home called Glenwood Canyon. Interstate 70 and a scenic bike trail wind through the canyon floor for roughly eighteen miles. The steep, extremely vertical canyon walls rise several thousand feet. The Colorado River rushes through the canyon floor. There are places where the water cascades over huge boulders with great force and velocity. The distinct boundaries of the canyon mark its beauty and power.

However, if you violate those boundaries it might just kill you. My dad and I saw that happen once to a group of people attempting to raft through an extremely dangerous section of the river in early spring. The classification system used in kayaking says that Class 5+

to Class 6 water is technically not navigable. That stretch of water is beyond Class 6 and is divided into two sections called "Upper Death" and "Lower Death" by kayaking and rafting enthusiasts.

We were driving through the canyon when we noticed four people in a raft come around a sharp bend. They were headed toward "Upper Death" where the water descended in raging torrents over massive boulders. We were incredulous that people would actually be foolish enough to attempt such a thing. The force of the water instantly folded the raft in half shooting the two people in the front out, as if they were pebbles being slung by a slingshot.

We quickly pulled the car over and raced down to the river well below the rapids. We could see two people periodically surface in the water only to disappear again. Incredibly, they made it through. They were extremely fortunate not to have been trapped beneath undercut rock and drowned. We were able to get out into the calm water below the rapids and help pull them to safety. Never have I seen two more frightened, hysterical people. They were truly lucky to be alive.

2
Boundary's Attributes

God uses boundaries to create power, focus and beauty. Those elements are all present in Glenwood Canyon.

There is power because the water is channeled in one direction. That gives it focus, which in turn creates both energy and beauty. Boundaries create a sense of order that should not be violated, like those rafters attempted to do.

The Bible tells us that all the boundaries of life are in the hands of God, and that includes more than simply geographic lines on a map. He has established the boundaries of the earth (Psalms 74:17); the nations and the times of their habitation (Acts 18:26); and even our individual genetic structure (Psalms 140:13-16).

In Chapter Four, I used the analogy that God was like a "Cosmic Secretary" writing our appointments for us in pencil and ink. Those appointments come to us in the context of our boundaries. They are appointments and boundaries at the same time.

The appointments/boundaries in ink we cannot affect. For instance, we are powerless to determine who our parents are, our gender or the times into which we are born.

However, it's possible to influence the appointments/boundaries that are written in pencil. By this, I am referring to such things as who we marry, the relationships we develop, where we work or where we live.

God intends for these appointments/boundaries to make our lives more ordered, powerful, focused and beautiful. But when we tamper with our penciled-in appointments/boundaries, our destiny can be badly compromised. It's like the phrase that's used in the intelligence community and that we hear so often in espionage movies: this represents a "clear and present danger." It's readily possible to muck up your life if you're not careful. Therefore, it's imperative that we have a submissive attitude when it comes to those appointments/boundaries written in pencil. We must trust God that they are being used for our well-being.

3
A Disaster Waiting to Happen

Why do we periodically make decisions that are self-destructive? There are many possible reasons. I think of them as culprits, erroneous beliefs, feelings or desires that rob me of a life of joy, purpose and fruitfulness. They are not an external force. Unlike other culprits, their attacks come from within. I can be my own worst enemy.

Once, I had an experience with boundaries that demonstrated many of the mistakes people make that bring about serious consequences. It's another story about aquatic misadventures, this time my own.

When I was a teenager, my best friend and I heard stories about the excitement of canoe floating. We imagined ourselves gliding through rapids, enjoying the thrill of feeling the water splash about us. So we talked our fathers into taking us on a float trip. It seemed innocent enough, but the trip was a disaster and could have cost us our lives.

The first problem was that my dad and I knew absolutely nothing about the sport. But, as so many people falsely reason, how difficult could it be? After all, we were somewhat athletic and pretty smart guys. We'd figure it out.

So, we took a leap of faith, assuming everything would be fine. This in realty was not faith, but presumption. We later learned that there's a big difference between the two.

Our faith in ourselves led to several serious errors. Fundamentally, we didn't plan wisely or take the necessary precautions. The smart thing to do when you canoe float is to wrap all your supplies in plastic and then tie them to the canoe with rope. We saw that as a lot of unnecessary effort. The river was supposed to be fairly innocuous, and we would steer clear of any possible danger. Before we embarked, our companions encouraged us to take those precautions, just in case something happened. We didn't listen to their advice.

The first few days went well. We got the feel of handling the canoe and navigated our way through several difficult rapids. This bolstered our confidence to the point of cockiness, thinking we could handle about anything the river threw at us.

It was just as my friend and I had envisioned. The natural beauty, paired with the excitement of the fast moving water, was thrilling. Plus, it was fun to leisurely fish the river as we floated between the rapids.

Ultimately, our newfound confidence didn't serve us well. We came to one particularly challenging stretch of water where two huge boulders created a narrow chute that channeled the water's powerful flow into a cliff wall. The wall then turned the water sharply to the left. Immediately to the side of the rapid was a beautiful, deep pool that we were certain contained many fish.

We should have been content to just get through the rapid, but the pool was too enticing. So we turned the canoe around and headed back up stream, staying within the calm water of the pool. Dad wanted me to fish the water beneath the cliff wall at the point where the water started to slow down and collect at the base of the pool.

We simply didn't appreciate how dangerous and powerful the water was. We soon learned. As we tried to maneuver the canoe into just the right spot, we got a little too flirtatious with the rapid. Quickly, the water spun the canoe in a counter-clockwise direction.

We tried to counter the force, but it was too strong. We were thrown into the cliff wall. The rushing current forced the canoe to capsize.

Out we went into the chilly spring-fed river. The force was so strong that we didn't even submerge. Instead, we were pushed against the canoe, half in and half out of the water. The force of the water trapped the canoe against the cliff wall.

The water pounded us as we struggled to breathe. Then, Dad got a startled look on his face, took a quick breath and was sucked under. The current shot the canoe out the back end of the rapid. I was able to hold on to the canoe and let it pull me out with it. Dad resurfaced gasping for air about ten yards further downstream.

Luckily, the capsized canoe floated into him, and we were both able to hang on. Finally, we reached shore about seventy-five yards past the rapid.

All of our food, clothes, camping equipment and fishing supplies were gone. The items that sank immediately were somewhere beneath the rapid. The water was too deep to allow us to retrieve anything. Other items were swept far downstream.

By God's grace, we were able to retrieve several valuable items. Our two sleeping bags and the oars got tangled up in thick, over-hanging branches further downstream. Plus, our plastic cooler holding some of our food and drinks washed ashore.

The experience had been frightening. But as our friends approached the scene, the event took on another whole dimension. The fear was replaced by humiliation. First, we explained what happened, and they responded with courteous comments about our safety. Soon the conversation drifted to the realities of the situation. Some sharp words were exchanged, as our friends realized how our foolishness affected them. We had a long way to go, and now their food had to be split between the four of us. Plus, we had to stop for at least a day and build fires to dry out the sleeping bags.

It took an extra few days, but we got through the trip. Sadly, those were tension-filled days, tension created by our foolish actions. Needless to say, that was the last canoe float we ever took with my best friend and his father. What we do has implications for those around us.

4
The Culprit: An Uncontrolled Imagination

When it comes to relating to the boundaries of life, most of the culprits that can trip us up are present in my canoe story.

It started with my imagination, which fuelled my desires. Sometimes we allow ourselves to think on subjects that are not so innocent as a canoe trip. Consequently, our imaginations can be culprits that create images, desires and expectations that are not true of life.

An overly active imagination can romanticize a person, place or a situation, thereby enticing us to tamper with a penciled-in appointment/boundary. For instance, illicit sexual relationships typically start with an imagination not under the control of the Holy Spirit. Inevitably, the boundary of God's law is violated, and havoc results.

We can do this same thing with places. We are fortunate to live in a beautiful place. Many times we've seen people move to the mountains, thinking the wonderful surroundings are all they need to be happy. Then, after a brief period of "mountain euphoria," they realize that their problems moved here with them.

Career moves can be the same way. We can make changes, fantasizing that the new situation will be far better than the current one. It might be. Or we might be running away from problems. The issue could be that we don't understand what God is trying to teach us in our existing situation.

A friend tells an amusing story regarding this truth, although it wasn't funny to him or his family when it happened. He had requested a transfer because he had a strong personality conflict with his immediate supervisor.

The organization accommodated his request. Then, after a few years in the new assignment, the same thing happened. They moved again. Then, after a few years, he experienced the same kinds of tensions with others.

In his mind these relational conflicts had always been the other person's fault. He reasoned that it was just his bad luck to have this happen to him three times. He always thought things would be better at the next job.

He hated his current job and had a miserable relationship with his boss. However, he was concerned for his family. The disruption from multiple moves had taken an obvious toll on them. This time he moved a little slower and prayed about whether he should make another change.

Then one day, as he was contemplating the potential move, a strange thought flashed into his mind. "You can move again, but I have another boss just like this one waiting for you."

That seemed like an unusual notion, he thought. Where did it come from? Perhaps it was a thought from God. This was disconcerting because it implied that maybe the problem was his and not another's. This caused him to take an introspective look at his own attitudes.

In addition, he sought counsel from his peers. The jury's verdict was unanimous. It was obvious to everyone that he struggled with submission to authority. No one had said anything because he was unapproachable, defiant and blind to his fault.

He decided to stick with the situation, and, as a result, he overcame the character flaw. He became a better man, and that ugly attribute lost its ability to rob him of joy, purpose and fruitfulness.

Some people have to be in control, or they simply can't function. Important appointments can be compromised because of that. My friend used to be this kind of person. But now he can follow anyone.

5
The Culprit: An Unteachable Spirit

Our lack of willingness to listen to counsel was another culprit on the canoe float. How often do we decide to launch off in some direction, refusing to listen to counsel. Sometimes we get our wish and a lot of misery in the process.

Many times in business I've seen people take jobs that for one reason or another weren't well-suited for them. Employees would come to me asking for advice. Shortly into such conversations, it would be readily apparent they didn't want advice at all. Their minds were already made up. What they really wanted was validation for a decision they had already made.

Forces are at work within us, and they hold us firmly in their grasp. Sometimes it's a psychological desire for recognition. Other times it's a need to prove something to a parent or the family or our peer group. These psychological forces prompt us to make moves that might not be in our best interest.

One of God's fundamental tools of protection, designed to steer us away from bad thinking, is wise counsel. But do we listen?

My experience with legitimate God-ordained transitions is that there is a harmony and consistency between the different factors involved in the change. There is not a spirit of confusion. There is, instead, a kindred spirit.

Typically four variables line up. Those four variables are my inner convictions, guidance from scripture, counsel and circumstances. If they don't align themselves then it's a signal that maybe I should re-evaluate my contemplated change. I've not always been led to pleasant appointments. But I've believed I was where I was supposed to be because of the alignment of those four variables.

For instance, if the counsel I receive is not consistent, it raises a "red flag." I sense that something's not right. Perhaps God is trying to protect me from a mistake.

Also, don't get counsel from just anyone. Search for wise, mature and knowledgeable people. I've seen people arrange counsel from only those people who they know will tell them what they want to hear. Always get the right counsel, well equipped to address the subject at hand.

When the four variables line up, a tremendous thing happens. There is peace. That's important because it's inevitable that problems will occur. There is comfort, reassurance and strength in knowing you're exactly where you're supposed to be, to know you're not running from something. Then, we can be assured that the problems we encounter are serving a purpose. God is using them to create value and spiritual substance.

6

The Culprit: Being Manipulative

If Dad were alive today, he would agree with me that manipulation is a strong family trait. We both manifested it on the float trip. We had to have our way.

Keeping my hands off of penciled-in appointments/boundaries has always proved difficult. That's because I'm a certified Type-A. When I err, it's from being too aggressive, not too laid back. That can be a problem because it means I have ideas about how things should play out. I'm going to do whatever I can to make things work out my way.

A good friend of mine at The Navigators, who also was a recovering Type-A, saw this tendency in me years ago. He did me a great favor by addressing the issue and giving me a way of controlling the problem, so that I couldn't do myself harm in the future.

This happened one day over lunch. We were discussing this problem, when he suggested that perhaps I should consider taking a vow of obscurity. What did he mean, I asked? We talked about the concept of vows and then he took his Bible and opened it to the following passage from Isaiah:

> ...The Lord called me before my birth; from within the womb He called me by name. He made my words of judgment as sharp as a sword. He has hidden me in the shadow of His hand. I am like a sharp arrow in His quiver. He said to me, 'You are my servant, Israel, and you will bring Me glory.' I replied, 'But my work all seems so useless! I have spent my strength for nothing and to no purpose at all. Yet, I leave it all in the Lord's hand; I will trust God for my reward.' [135]

The principles in this verse have application beyond Isaiah and Israel, to whom they are addressed. As we discussed the passage my friend explained that it was enough to be content in God's quiver. It was up to God to decide if, when, and how He would use my life. Reward was found in obedience not in public visibility.

Taking a vow of obscurity was, in effect, saying to God: "You take the initiative regarding my penciled-in *appointments* and *boundaries*. I will try to live faithfully within the context of my current situation. You have allowed my situation to be. You can change it if You choose. Meanwhile, I'll focus on obedience and try to learn the lessons You have for me in my circumstances.

I'll analyze new opportunities that come across my path believing by faith that You might wish to change a *boundary* in my life. But I will wait in my existing circumstance trusting You to confirm, guide and lead."

A vow of obscurity means refusing to canvas for recognition, promotion or change. It means choosing to submit to the unreasonable boss or remain in an assignment I would like to leave. It might mean staying in a relationship I otherwise wish would end. It could mean living in a certain place for the rest of my life.

The conversation made sense to me. Here was something I could do to address my tendency to manipulate. I could simply vow to take my hands off things. If God was who I believed He was, then He was more than capable of leading me to legitimate change.

When I have observed the vow (and sadly I haven't always), it's protected me. It's kept me from making decisions that would have proven to be big mistakes. It's given me strong confidence that I'm securely living in God's will for my life. That, in turn, has provided me with strength during tough times. And lastly, it's given me a clear conscience and purified my motives, because I know I'm not doing something as a result of my manipulative tendencies.

7
The Culprit: Lack of Contentment

Often we tamper with an appointment/boundary because we lack contentment. My father and I just couldn't leave that dangerous rapid and its alluring pool alone. Sometimes things can be clearly dangerous, but we want to cross the boundary and reach for it anyway.

Jesus' life provides an amazing model that illustrates important truths about contentment as it relates to the appointments and boundaries in our lives.

Jesus also had penciled-in appointments/boundaries with which He could have tampered. But He never did. His public ministry commenced when He was about thirty years old and was signaled through His baptism by John the Baptist.

Commenting on this occasion, Matthew 3:17 says:

...and behold, a voice out of the heavens saying, 'This is my beloved Son in whom I am well pleased.' [136]

I'll reiterate this point. What had Jesus done up to this time in His life to elicit such an incredible compliment from God the Father? We can only conclude from the Bible that he had done three things. One, He had been a carpenter, (Mark 6:3). Two, He subjected Himself to the authority of His earthly parents, (Luke 2:52). And three, He grew up in wisdom and stature before God and men, (Luke 2:52).

His public ministry lasted roughly three years. This means that Jesus spent approximately ninety percent of His life in relative obscurity. It's amazing that He did not chafe at those long and obscure years, but rather submitted to them in a spirit of obedience. That was the attitude that God the Father was praising when John baptized Jesus. He had done nothing but be a carpenter and a dutiful son.

Oswald Chambers wrote:

We are so busy telling God where we would like to go. The man or woman who is really for God and His work is the one who carries off the prize when the summons comes. We wait with the idea of some great opportunity, something sensational, and when it comes we are quick to say, 'Here am I.' But we are not ready for an obscure duty. Readiness for God means we are ready for the tiniest little thing or the great big thing, it makes no difference. [137]

8
The Culprit: Faith vs. Presumption

A particularly dangerous culprit is not recognizing the difference between faith and presumption. When we got into that canoe, we had a blind faith in ourselves. Therefore, we presumed that everything would be fine. Often faith is really misguided presumption. We decide to do something, and then expect God to bless it.

Trusting God with the direction of our lives is one thing, but presuming upon Him is quite another. Presumption expects or even demands the blessing of God, whereas faith is centered in a desire to yield to His Spirit's guidance. With faith, we are people of initiative but with one important qualifier—submission to the Spirit's will.

Proverbs 16:9 says: "The mind of man plans his way, **but** the Lord directs his steps." [138] Hence, human initiative and divine guidance work together to confirm the *appointments* and *boundaries* of our lives. That only works with an attitude of submission.

I like to visualize this truth by likening my life to a ship. God cannot guide me if I stay securely anchored to the pier, in some safe harbor in my life. But, if I loose the lines and venture out into sea, then He can guide me. I have to be willing to steer the vessel in the direction He dictates.

There are mistakes to avoid at opposite ends of the spectrum. One, I don't want to race ahead of the Holy Spirit's guidance in a willful way, steering the ship in whatever direction I please. And secondly, I don't want to lag behind in a spirit of fear, keeping the ship close to the safety of the harbor. Sometimes God says "move out," and we need to do so with faith and enthusiasm.

I've made the mistake of not recognizing the difference between faith and presumption. I once undertook an endeavor that violated this principle. I "moved out" when God hadn't instructed me to do so, and I paid a high price for the mistake. This mistake is closely related to the previous principle I discussed of being manipulative. We can want something, put a spiritual spin on a particular situation, and then assume God will bless our decisions which in reality are outside His will for our lives.

This was especially sad because I knew better. I violated the vow of obscurity and was not content in my circumstances. Both mistakes led me to presume upon God's blessing.

Here's what happened. Wonderful things occurred as a result of my experience at the Pyxis Corporation. Those were wonderful days for us. Our kids were grown, and as empty-nesters, we had new found freedom. We now had the time and resources to do some of the things we had always dreamed of. We took advantage of the opportunity and traveled extensively.

The success at Pyxis created visibility in the business community. Consequently, I was presented with numerous business opportunities. I found one to be particularly enticing. I had been asked to become CEO of a company that applied "point of use" technologies like Pyxis to industries outside of healthcare.

Something else was happening at the time that affected my thinking. It was early in 2000 and the "tech bubble" was starting to burst. Between March of 2000 and October of 2002, the country experienced the worst market crash since The Great Depression. Stocks lost roughly fifty percent of their value, or close to seven trillion dollars. Like most Americans, we were feeling the impact of that event. I was concerned about our financial well-being.

So I took the job, and it was several years of misery. At first things went well. I was full of confidence. I'd done this before, and I understood the technology. I had no reason to believe we wouldn't be successful.

Then the catastrophic event occurred—9/11. Few things in the national life have had such an impact as that disaster. It certainly affected business. We watched capital acquisitions come to a screeching halt, while businesses assessed their situations in light of this event.

But I had a problem that I did not recognize. I'm convinced that one of the hardest things to do in life is handle prosperity. It came our way, and we failed the test miserably. The early American clergyman, Cotton Mather, rightly warned: "Unless there was vigilance, a sense of calling would bring forth prosperity, only to result in prosperity's destroying the sense of calling." [139]

My problem handling prosperity started with genuine fatigue mixed with self-pity. We had worked hard. Why not relax for a while? Plus, it was easy to be prideful, taking more credit than we deserved for success. That led to laxity and a subtle compromise of the Biblical principles that created the success originally.

I suppose some characteristics can be both strengths and weaknesses. That's the case with me. I have always been ambitious and aggressive. At times those traits have served me well. But in this instance, they were weaknesses.

It's not worth going into many of the details of those troubled years. Suffice it to say that the company struggled. The situation degenerated into a lawsuit with disgruntled investors which eventually settled in arbitration.

Although it was a complicated situation, rightly or wrongly, I received much criticism and blame for these events. My reputation was tarnished, and the experience was personally humiliating. Relationships I had valued became strained. It was several years of confrontations, threats and accusations.

We suffered significant financial loss. That was ironic, because we had undertaken the endeavor to avoid just that. I would have been far better off financially if I'd never taken the position.

Thankfully, it finally came to an end. We retreated to our home in Colorado, a place we virtually had not seen for two years, and tried to assess why all this had happened.

What had I done wrong? I spent the better part of a year trying to understand this. Herein is the value of sober-mindedness that we discussed in Chapter Eight. We had a record of the evolution of our hearts. It was recorded in our journals. We spent long hours recounting our thoughts and feelings during that period.

Two things became readily apparent to us as we studied our journals. First, we realized that we had gone to Pyxis for the right reasons. We had sincerely wanted to live out the reality of our relationship with Christ in the context of business. However, although there were platitudes to that effect in our journals, it was obvious we had not gone to this more recent assignment for the same reasons. Pyxis had been about God's glory; this assignment had been about my glory—a motivation God never promises to honor. Brutal honesty required me to admit that my main motivation was greed.

Secondly, the journals revealed a real flaw in the process we went through in coming to that decision. Although many of the things I'm addressing in this chapter were present, one was glaringly absent. Guidance from scripture was not present. When we went to Pyxis, we had page after page of Biblical insights and instructions that tended to confirm God's leading. But there wasn't any of that regarding this recent decision.

Sometimes our reasoning process can be our worst enemy. It seemed logical. I knew the technology. There was a good management team in place. The company was well-funded. I liked the Board of Directors. The market need was obvious. What was missing? The calling of God was missing!

I had created an appointment/boundary that I thought was right for me. In the final analysis, I crossed the line between faith and presumption. I had falsely reasoned that God had called me to that appointment. He had not.

However, God used my mistake to bring about good things. In His grace, He taught us much about prosperity, contentment and walking before Him in contriteness. It is part of His genius and kindness to take a tampered-with appointment/boundary and use it for good.

9
Wolff's Law, or How We Grow Spiritually

Some of my friend's comments regarding the vow of obscurity in Isaiah 49:2-4 were hard to take but were important nonetheless. He said our job was to focus on the process of becoming "select arrows" in God's quiver. We all have different talents and different needs. God takes us through a unique process designed exclusively for us so we can become "select arrows."

This process reminded me of a law of physics called Wolff's Law, with which I was familiar. Wolff's Law is a key principle utilized in orthopedic surgery. It says that for growth to take place, there needs to be stress. Hence, if an orthopedic implant doesn't stress surrounding bone, re-vascularization does not occur, i.e. blood supply is lost. If that happens, the bone atrophies.

In like manner, God's appointments and boundaries sometimes stress us so we can grow spiritually. We need to submit to that process, not subvert it.

10
Submitting to Boundaries

Have you ever noticed that most of the failures recorded in the Bible are stories about people who somehow refused to submit to a God-ordained appointment or boundary? The Kings of Israel are good examples.

Once I created a chronological time line of the Kings. In it, I noted their primary successes and failures. Although there were a few exceptions, most of their reigns are considered failures. Why?

Interestingly, virtually all of the cases of failure could serve as examples for the subject of this chapter—the importance of not usurping God's authority by tampering with penciled-in appointment/boundaries. Kings failed because they weren't content or wouldn't listen to counsel or presumed upon God or had wrong desires fueled by imaginations that were out of control.

Even King David, although generally considered a great king, was not immune to such mistakes. He created much pain for himself by gazing at the beautiful Bathsheba while she bathed. His imagination and lack of contentment then led him to violate numerous boundaries. Those actions would plague him for the rest of his life.

For the most part, David was a man who allowed God to be God of all his appointments/boundaries. He was a man who walked by true faith and did not presume upon God.

He refused to usurp God's authority even when his enemies were within his grasp, as when he spared King Saul's life in the cave at

Engedi (I Samuel 24). Although he had been told he would be the next King of Israel, David waited for that appointment to come to him. He did not tamper with it, but waited for God to act.

David got it right. He serves as a man to emulate. God pays David the highest compliment, calling him a man who followed Him with all his heart (I Kings 14:8). David was a man of action and took much initiative when it came to placing faith in God. He saw a huge God capable of anything. He clearly demonstrated this attitude in his encounter with Goliath (I Samuel 17).

We get insight into his attitudes by studying his prayer in Psalm 131:

> O Lord, my heart is not proud, nor my eyes haughty; nor do I involve myself in great matters, or in things too difficult for me; surely I have composed and quieted my soul; like a weaned child rests against his mother, my soul is like a weaned child within me. [140]

David didn't strive to be somebody he wasn't or do something that wasn't intended for him. He was comfortable letting go and allowing God to assign him a place, a role in life that was perfect for him. His focus instead was making sure his soul was rightly related to his God—like a weaned child resting against its mother.

11
Concluding Thoughts

Section Three has dealt with three specific things we can do that will help us experience more joy, purpose and fruitfulness in life.

Becoming sober-minded people and living for others require action and initiative on our parts. These are things we willfully grasp. Submitting to boundaries requires just the opposite. Our willful action is to let go and trust God. The boundaries are in our lives for a reason. If we trust God within them, they will make us more powerful, focused and spiritually-oriented people.

However, there's an exception to this rule. There may be times when we should take initiative regarding changing a boundary. If we are ever placed in compromising situations where we are asked to do something that is illegal or immoral, then we need to make a change. It's far more important to submit to a higher boundary—God's law.

3
Action Steps

Responding to the Boundaries of Life • from Chapter Ten

As was discussed in Chapter Four, appointments can be written in ink or pencil. These appointments can also form boundaries in our lives. The ink boundaries cannot be changed. In dealing with the ink boundaries we will focus on our abilities. The pencil boundaries include such things as our choice of being single or married, where we live, what we choose as our career, etc. The pencil boundaries can be tampered with.

A boundary does more than one thing at a time, for it may limit you in one area but protect you in another. Regardless of whether they are written in ink or pencil, they are divine appointments by God that create order by putting everything in its place in time.

Thou hast established all the boundaries of the earth...
—**Psalms 74:17**

...and He made from one, every nation of mankind to live on all the face of the earth, having determined their appointed times, and the boundaries of their habitations...
—**Acts 18:26**

For Thou didst form my inward parts...and in Thy book they were all written, the days that were ordained for me, when as yet there was not one of them.   —**Psalms 140:13-16**

28. Using the ink and pencil appointments from Query #15 (on page 114), which appointments have formed boundaries in your life? Feel free to add others to this list. Place a check mark by any boundary that you struggle with.

Ink boundaries:

○ _____

○ _____

○ _____

Pencil boundaries:

○ _____

○ _____

○ _____

29. Several "culprits" can cause problems with our pencilled boundaries: an uncontrolled imagination, an unteachable spirit, being manipulative, lack of contentment and faith vs. presumption.

I have tried to tamper with a pencil boundary by doing:

_____

_____

_____

30. God uses the "Wolff's Law" stresses of life to reshape our thinking and values that strengthen us spiritually. "Living in obscurity" means to intentionally not interfere in this process. Among other positive results, "living in obscurity" allows God to purify our motives.

Some desires, tendencies, and behavioral patterns that keep me from "living in obscurity" are:

_____

_____

If I were to observe the principle of "living in obscurity," here is a situation I'm involved in right now that I should leave alone:

_____

_____

_____

I can see now that God may be using this current situation in my life to make me grow spiritually in this area:

_____

_____

_____

Here is a personal prayer I can use to ask God to help me "live in obscurity":

Lord, You take the initiative in my boundaries because I refuse to exercise mine. I don't care if this is written in pencil or ink. It may be temporary, or it may be permanent. It doesn't matter. I will submit and embrace what is before me. You allowed this into my life, and You can take it away if You desire. I choose to learn and grow from this. I will come to experience the satisfaction of understanding your purpose. Therefore, I refuse to canvas for recognition, promotion or change. I choose to submit to the unreasonable boss, stay in an assignment I would naturally like to avoid, continue in a relationship that I wish would end, not take the initiative with a relationship that I desire, or vow to live in this place for the rest of my life. I will analyze new opportunities that cross my path believing by faith that you might possibly want to change the boundaries in my life. But, also, by faith I will wait in existing circumstances trusting you to confirm and guide.

Or, *I need to pray about this situation in light of what I have learned from the exercises on boundaries, keeping in mind the idea of "living in obscurity":*

_____

_____

_____

_____

_____

_____

_____

_____

_____

_____

_____

_____

_____

_____

_____

_____

_____

_____

_____

_____

SECTION FOUR
Enjoying the Fruits of Your Labor

Wrestling with your destiny, or responding appropriately to the appointments in your life, will produce results, not only in eternity, but right now. What could the impact be if you apply the principles we've discussed throughout the book? I've referred to joy, purpose and fruitfulness. Let's look at what joy, purpose and fruitfulness might look like.

• • • •

"The Christian must carry his religion into everything…[it] makes a man a better commander, a better shoemaker, a better tailor. It teaches him punctuality, fidelity…in the command of an army, it calms his perplexities at a critical hour."

—General Thomas "Stonewall" Jackson
Civil War Military Commander

CHAPTER ELEVEN
The Integrated Life:
Experiencing the Purposes of God

1

Connectedness

A great delight for Kathy and me is being grandparents. Part of that joy is watching our children be parents. I am especially amazed at the intuitive sense our daughters-in-law have for their children. They can be in different rooms and somehow sense what their kids are up to elsewhere in the house. It's as if they have internal radar that senses trouble if it's near. Sometimes this intuitive sense is roused by the noises they hear. Other times it can be triggered by silence. Regardless, they are in touch with their children's lives, fully intent on loving and protecting them. They are connected to their kids in a mystical and loving way.

I've noticed that this connectedness is bi-directional. That is, our grandchildren crave to be watched, played with, comforted and protected. They love knowing someone's there guarding them and that they are not alone.

Recently, I spent time with our granddaughter, Misha. We were playing with building blocks on the living room floor, but then a book caught her attention. Typically, she wants me to read to her, but not this time. She wanted to play like she was reading. She simply wanted to know I was there watching her read. As she held the book upside down, she would periodically glance up at me to see if I was paying attention to her.

Needless to say, such things can melt a grandfather's heart. It made me think that perhaps we bring the same kind of joy to God's heart as He watches us earnestly wrestle with our destinies before Him—diligently seeking to make the most of our appointments in life.

Connectedness implies sensing the love and presence of God and feeling the spiritual purpose behind the events that make up our lives. It is having an integrated life. To integrate means to bring all the parts together, to unify. It seems to me that no one wants to live a disconnected, fragmented, compartmentalized life, a life where they cannot sense a connectedness to the purposes of God.

If you think of a house as a metaphor for your life, connectedness would be like sensing what's going on in all the rooms of your house at the same time. The opposite would be sensing only what was happening in the room you are currently occupying.

For example, in the early days of my Christian experience, Christ was present in all the rooms of my house, but I didn't recognize His presence. I sensed Him in my Sunday morning church room, and I sensed Him in my Wednesday night Bible study room. But I wasn't aware of His presence in my Monday through Friday work rooms.

To be overly compartmentalized also means to be insensitive to the linkages between the various rooms of our houses. In this case, the rooms refer to our fundamental roles in life. For instance, I once knew a man who was so compartmentalized that he actually made his wife schedule appointments to see him if she needed to talk to him on a business day. I can well imagine how that made her feel. His life was compartmentalized, and all the parts were segregated from each other. He was insensitive to the linkage between his role as a business leader and husband.

I knew another man whose life was so one dimensional, that after retirement, his family actually asked him to go back to work, saying: "We have learned how to live without you."

So pursuing the goals we have discussed in the book can transform us into lay people with integrated lives. By that, I mean we become aware that Christ is present and working in every area of our lives. He's in every room and we know it. We sense purpose in all the things we do and in every relationship.

I've referred often in the book to seeking joy, purpose and fruitfulness. Living an integrated life, being fully aware of your connectedness to God does much to enhance those three qualities.

Theologian Paul Helm writes, "The goal and end of a person's calling does not terminate in this life, but it makes sense only in the light of the life to come...The basic fact about the present life is that it is important and valuable in all its aspects because it leads to the world to come." [141]

Randy Alcorn elaborated on this thought when he wrote: "The world to come is what we were made for—and it gives shape and meaning to our present lives." [142] That's connectedness.

2
The Man Who Found Connectedness

While at Pyxis I had a colleague who was especially mature and competent. Consequently, the company promoted him to a major leadership role in the organization. However, he struggled in his new role and asked to be moved back into his old assignment.

I was surprised and asked him why. He proceeded to tell me how frustrated he felt as a vice-president. It seemed that most of his days were full of conflict resolution. He went on to say that he didn't like who he was becoming and referenced his increasingly bitter, negative attitude. He had concluded that management wasn't well suited to him, and that he'd be better off moving back into a more independent role.

My colleague was a Christian but one with a compartmentalized view of life. He didn't recognize Jesus Christ's presence in the "business room" of his house, and that mistake was robbing him of joy and purpose.

He was making the mistake that Randy Alcorn was referring to when he wrote: "How many times have we prayed that God would make us Christlike, then begged him to take us from the very things he sent to make us Christlike. How many times has God heard our cries when we imagined he didn't? How many times has he said no to our prayers when saying yes would have harmed us and robbed us of good?" [143]

My colleague had a solid faith, so we could talk openly about the possible spiritual realities hidden behind his earthly experience. I asked him what he thought God wanted most for our lives. He paused momentarily and said: "I suppose He wants to conform us to the image of Jesus Christ." Then we talked for a moment about what that meant in reality.

He mentioned that one of the things he respected most about Christ was His unconditional love. I thought about that and said, "How better to create that trait than to surround us with unlovely people and unlovely situations? If things were always positive and upbeat, how would a Christian ever become unconditionally loving like Jesus? Perhaps you are actually in a position of honor before God. It seems He cares enough about you to give you the experiences that will make you a man of unconditional love."

We talked about how there is always spiritual reality behind our experiences but that we tend not to recognize them. He concluded that those difficult experiences were actually integral to his development as a man and a Christian.

The conversation convicted him and it brought him to a defining moment. He vowed to stay in his position and endeavor to view it differently. He chose to focus on Christ and not his struggles. This enabled him to see the purposes of God behind those struggles and extract spiritual value from them. In his mind, he now had a stewardship to honor and a trust to keep, rather than problems to run away from.

He stayed in that position for several years and enjoyed much success. In the process, he demonstrated true leadership skills and became respected as one who truly cared for and nurtured those under his authority.

Bearing fruit in life occurs in two ways: first, in the development of our character and second, in enhancing the spiritual lives of others. Both of those things became true for my colleague. He found connectedness and enjoyed experiencing an integrated life.

3
Pyxis and Connectedness

My colleague's experience at Pyxis was not dissimilar from my own. Remember, I talked about God's values and rewards centering around character and characters. Then I also talked about doing something with God before doing something for God.

Both of us, through our positions at Pyxis, wanted to grow in character and do things with Jesus. That meant trying to lead like He would lead, make decisions like He would make decisions and approach situations like He would approach situations. That meant communicating and trying to be sensitive to His promptings on a daily basis.

When that happens, it automatically leads to influencing the characters around us.

4
All of Life is Holy

Oswald Chambers said: "Never allow the thought 'I am of no use where I am;' because you certainly are of no use where you are not." [144]

We do not recognize the spiritual value of the moment. As a result, it can be easy to be discontented and have no peace regarding our circumstances. These sentiments often make us feel like we need to do something rash, such as change jobs or live somewhere else. But in reality, all of life is holy and meant to be lived in intimate fellowship with Christ. That enables us to do things with God on a moment-by-moment basis, rather than thinking we need to do something for God. There is a subtle yet profound difference between *with* God and *for* God.

God wants my fellowship, not my production. If I'm in fellowship with Him, my life will naturally produce fruit for Him. Understanding and living by this truth creates a calming effect, allowing me to relax and enjoy my relationship with Christ. All the parts of my life will be connected or integrated around my relationship with Christ. My self-awareness is replaced by Christ-awareness. Instead of being pre-occupied with self and my feelings, I become focused on the spiritual value of the moment and what God is accomplishing in my life that will conform me to the image of Christ.

Feeling compelled to do something for Christ, without understanding the principle of integration, leads to a guilt trip, because we don't recognize the spiritual purpose in our existing circumstances.

Again, grandparenting has taught us much about this truth. Our first desire is to be with our grandchildren, to enjoy them and share their lives. The time with them naturally makes us want to do things for them. So we find ourselves encouraging them, teaching them, protecting them and buying things for them that they need or might enjoy. But we view every moment, regardless of what it may be, as a valuable moment.

5

A Simple Man, a Simple Task, a Profound Destiny

There are many people I'm anxious to meet in eternity. There's one man in particular that I want to thank for the unique contribution he made to my life. He lived in Europe over 300 years ago and was a simple cook in a monastery.

His name was Brother Lawrence. He spent most of his time doing a simple task, washing pots and pans with God. But he also managed to find time to write about the experience. He penned a short book destined to become a Christian classic entitled, *The Practice of the Presence of God.*

The book radiates joy, purpose and fruitfulness. It's obvious when you read Brother Lawrence that you are witnessing a man deeply in love with Christ. God was not some vague, distant theological concept to him.

He says many profound things in the book. However, several of his observations stand out. One of his thoughts was that he focused on doing the little things well, because he didn't see himself capable of doing big things.

Another one was that he didn't think about rewards at all. Knowing Christ and sensing His presence daily was reward enough. That reality caused this humble monk to wash pots and pans to the best of his ability.

This was a man with a connected, integrated life. He was a man who responded wisely to his appointments in life and consequently had a profound destiny. It's encouraging to realize that's possible for all lay people, regardless of our stations in life.

Oswald Chambers said: "Some people do a certain thing and the way in which they do it hallows that thing forever afterwards. It may be the most commonplace thing, but after we have seen them do it, it becomes different. When the Lord does a thing through us, He always transfigures it." [145]

4

Enjoying the Fruits of Your Labor

*The Integrated Life: Experiencing
the Purposes of God • from Chapter Eleven*

If you think of a house as a metaphor for your life, connectedness would be like sensing what's going on in all the rooms of your house at the same time.

31. The following is a simple floor plan. Think of each room as a separate compartment of your life (such as family, friends, business, church, neighborhood, hobbies, etc.) and label them accordingly. If you need more rooms, just add them on.

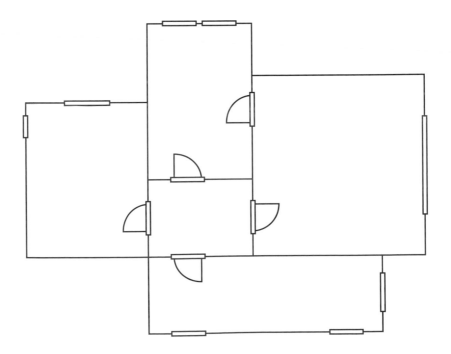

32. The opposite of being connected would be to live a disconnected, fragmented and compartmentalized life.

If I am to live an integrated life, here is what I need to do to bring all the parts of my life together, connected by the love and purposes of God:

_____

_____

_____

_____

_____

_____

_____

_____

_____

_____

_____

_____

_____

_____

_____

CHAPTER TWELVE
The Passionate Life:
Experiencing the Zeal of Christ

1
People and Passion

As I sat writing recently, my wife received what turned out to be a most gratifying phone call from our oldest son Mark. I couldn't help but be distracted as I listened to her animated responses to his comments.

Mark pursued a career in banking and is an officer with a banking system in Colorado. He was telling his mother how much he loved his job and how the days seemed to fly by. He went on to say that he felt positively challenged by the various aspects of his job.

Such things were gratifying to hear because it hasn't always been so for Mark. Early in his career he struggled with work that was ill suited for him. In addition, he was married and a father. He worked bizarre hours just to make ends meet and to give him discretionary time to get his MBA degree. He virtually had no life for four years. Needless to say, this was painful for us to watch as parents and grandparents.

We certainly respected his efforts and were delighted to see all the hard work finally pay off. Now he was in a position that was well suited to his skills and was brimming with future opportunity. Best of all, he has discretionary time for his family—he now has a life.

After the call, we brewed a pot of coffee and discussed his comments. In reality, we were basking in the afterglow of Mark's contentment. Ironically, I had been writing the introduction to this chapter when Mark called. As we sat drinking our coffee and talking, it struck us that his remarks were the essence of what the chapter was about—living the passionate life.

All of us want to be energized by what we do. No one's interested in a life of drudgery. We don't want to do things simply because we have to, but because we're convicted that what we are doing is important. We want to be consumed by a destiny of significance.

2

Blowing the Whistle on Big Tobacco

We saw a good example of a passionate life recently. We have a weekly tradition of watching *60 Minutes* on Sunday evening while enjoying a light supper. The habit seems to mark the official start of the week.

One evening Mike Wallace interviewed Jeffrey Wigand, the maverick insider who blew the whistle on big tobacco. The litigation in the mid-1990s resulted in a judgment of $368 billion dollars against the tobacco industry.

Perhaps, you recall the movie about those events. It was entitled *The Insider* and starred Russell Crowe as Jeffrey Wigand. Here's an excerpt from the interview.

'You begin to come across as a self-righteous true believer,' says Wallace.

'I believe there's a wrong being done,' says Wigand. 'I believe I have the capacity and the knowledge to help right the wrong. And I want to do that. Now, you want to call it self-righteous. I want to call it passion.'

But passion has its price. Wigand earned $300,000 a year working for tobacco. Now, he makes $60,000 working against it. He says the stress from going public led his wife to divorce him. But today, his daughters love him for what he's doing—and he loves doing it.

'I don't think I've been this happy in a long time. I mean, I enjoy what I do, and I'm comfortable with myself,' says Wigand. 'Everyday, I know I'm doing something that makes a difference for another human being. And that makes you feel good.'

3
Jesus Lived a Passionate Life

Passion is defined as an emotion with compelling force. Closely related to passion is the word zeal. Zeal means to be consumed by something, to boil, to be hot, fervent and to have great feeling.

These are the qualities we see in Jesus when He drove the moneylenders from the temple in Jerusalem:

> ...and to those who were selling the doves He said, 'Take these things away; and stop making my Father's house a house of merchandise.' His disciples remembered that it was written, 'Zeal for Thy House will consume me.' [146]

Jesus manifested "emotion with compelling force." He seemed "to boil, be hot and fervent." What compelled Him to act in such a way? It was love for His Heavenly Father and for anything that affected His Father's affairs on earth, especially His Father's house. Our lives can manifest those same qualities.

4
Understanding the Process: The Convergence Principle

In addition to being a true blessing, passion plays a significant role in capturing a meaningful destiny. However, becoming people of passion doesn't happen overnight. It's a process.

God supernaturally uses our circumstances to align three important aspects in our life experience. When those three aspects are aligned, we become people of passion. I call this the Convergence Principle, an alignment of talents, desires and convictions.

Our talents refer to our actual giftedness and capabilities, not what we think we are good at, or what we think we might enjoy. There can be a big difference between the two.

I grew up thinking I would be a good lawyer. I was wrong. God knew I would be a lousy, frustrated lawyer. God used early failures to lead me toward the right path and clarify my thinking regarding what my true talents were.

Os Guinness, in *The Call* says: "God normally calls us along the lines of our giftedness, but the purpose of giftedness is stewardship and service, not selfishness." [147]

Desires refer to the true yearnings of our hearts. They are not shallow wants like a new car or a higher salary or a vacation in Europe. Again God uses the experiences of life to clarify what are our true desires. These are things like a nurse's desire to aid people who are suffering or a teacher's desire to pass the love of learning on to another or a homemaker's desire to care for home and family.

Our convictions are those core values and beliefs that we hold dear, believing they are critical to live appropriately. Again, God uses the events of life to sculpt the proper core values within us, like our example of Robert E. Lee and his conviction regarding duty.

Jeffrey Wigand has deep convictions about the harmful nature of tobacco. He truly desires to do something about the problem. And lastly, he has the talents to use addressing the issue. Talent, desire and conviction have converged in his life. He understands his calling. He is a man of passion.

The world tends to define people by what they do—you are what you do. Jeffrey Wigand seems to be taking a different approach that's representative of a better way. He's doing who he is.

5
Called vs. Driven

When the Convergence Principle is at work in our lives we live with passion. That has ramifications that accrue to our benefit. It enables us to live as called people, rather than driven people.

Gordon MacDonald, in *Ordering Your Private World*, makes an important distinction between a called person versus a driven person. He says that some people go through life being driven by external forces that have exerted a negative influence on them. These forces might be thoughtless, cruel words or actions, or external environments void of spiritual reality.

Such situations can create an internal need for external things. Perhaps it's a need for external recognition. Or maybe it's a need for an external reward like money. Such people are driven by fear and pressure, becoming workaholics who relentlessly push themselves or others to insure that their needs are met.

Called individuals, on the other hand, are motivated by internal forces. They interpret the events of their external world in light of the truth in scripture. Therefore, they are comforted and directed as they go through life's storms. This allows a person not to be so reactive to life's struggles.

Instead of having something to rectify or prove, such people are responding to the call from God that comes from their inner life, from their relationship to Jesus Christ. Consequently, they are operating within the context of a personal calling, one conceived in love. They are on a mission and have a stewardship to keep.

Instead of fear, there is peace. Instead of pressure, there is the relaxed pursuit of excellence. Instead of workaholism, there is balance.

6
Looking for Passion

Passion is something that only God can create in our lives. Again there are no magic formulas for how He does that. However, often you will see two dynamics present in the creation of passion. People experience defining moments, and those defining moments create compulsions that move them to action.

A defining moment in life is an experience that strikes a deep chord within us. God uses such times to change the direction of our life. Defining moments create a heightened sensitivity to our convictions, desires and talents, the three components of the convergence principle.

Defining moments cannot be created; they are sovereign appointments. They are random. They might be a momentous experience, or they might come to us in a quiet moment. Regardless, they are unique and personal to the individual. They are moments when we experience truth for our lives. God engineers these times, and only He knows how they will affect us emotionally. True defining moments always create compulsions that irresistibly call us to action. We see an example of this in the Bible when Paul said he was being "irresistibly drawn" [148] by the Holy Spirit to Jerusalem.

Compulsions make us feel that our lives will not be complete if we don't take action. We sense that, if we don't respond, we will forever question ourselves.

However, a word of caution is in order. It's easy for our fickle hearts to rationalize that a desire is a compulsion from God. Again, wise counsel is a safeguard that can protect us. We need mature people in our lives, people who care about us and will pray with us as we wrestle with such delicate issues.

In addition, compulsions are not always pleasant. That was the case with Paul. You will recall that he experienced many trials and afflictions in Jerusalem. But it's possible to have peace of heart and live with passion, even in trying times, if we are taking action with a true God-ordained compulsion.

7
A By-Pass Surgery That Repaired Two Hearts

I mentioned earlier in the book how God led me away from my aspirations to be a lawyer into my true calling in healthcare. What I didn't do was tell you how that happened. It was a defining moment leading to a compulsion that moved me to action. At that time I had absolutely no inkling about what I should do with my life. Plus, I was upset with God because He wasn't honoring my desires to go into law.

I was like Dustin Hoffman in the movie *The Graduate*. In the opening scene, he wanders around his parents' cocktail party with a lost, bewildered look on his face. His parents' friends congratulate him on his graduation and ask him what he intends to do, or in some cases, they tell him what he should do. It is obvious the interactions are making him even more confused and discouraged.

Ironically, deliverance came at one of my parents' dinner parties.

It was exactly the same situation. Thankfully, a friend of my parents' thought I had potential and suggested I go to work for him. He was in management for a major healthcare company and had an entry level sales position that might be right for me.

I was just out of the military, recently married and needed money. I reasoned that at least I could make some money, gain business experience and go to law school later.

I got the job, and my calling began, although I didn't realize it at the time. The corporation I worked for had developed a filter for the cardio-pulmonary by-pass machines for use during coronary by-pass surgeries. So, at age twenty-two, I found myself in surgical suites almost everyday, working with the pump technicians to incorporate the filters into their by-pass techniques.

Although I enjoyed the work, that's all it was to me—work. I didn't see it as a calling, and it certainly wasn't the stuff destiny was made of. That is until the day when a three-year-old girl was wheeled into an operating suite.

Typically, by-pass patients were elderly. But this was a beautiful, blonde little girl with vivid blue eyes who had a life-threatening defect in her heart wall.

My first thought was of Kathy, who had the same kinds of facial features. Kathy must have looked like that as a girl. Then I thought that, when we had children, they would probably look much the same.

I thought about how dangerous those procedures were. It was 1971, and coronary by-pass procedures were relatively new. Each operation posed significant risk for the patient. Always wanting to be a father, I began envisioning what my feelings would be if this child were mine.

That's when the defining moment began. Emotions started to well up within me. I felt sympathy for the child and could sense the anguish and fear the parents must be feeling out in the waiting area. Those places are depressing enough, even without something like this to endure.

I watched as the procedure began. That's always a particularly gruesome moment. It begins by using a high speed saw to cut open the patient's chest, splitting the breastbone, or sternum.

That was just too much for me, because I was in a position where I could see both the traumatic cut and her beautiful, little face at the same time. I struggled to maintain my composure for the rest of the surgery.

Thankfully, the operation was a success. Still caught up in the emotion of the moment, I asked the surgeon if I could accompany him to the waiting room and observe his interaction with the family from a discrete distance. He graciously honored my request, and I followed him to the waiting room.

That proved to be as emotionally difficult as the surgery. The doctor held the parents' hands and delivered the good news. Their responses were a combination of fear, anguish, strain, relief and joy, all at the same time.

My senses were on overload. I had to get out of the hospital and think about all that had transpired. I dressed quickly and went out to my car in the parking lot. It didn't take long until I was sobbing uncontrollably.

I was mentally bombarded by powerful new realizations. First of all, I was deeply impressed by the magnitude and importance of what had just happened. My respect for healthcare was born that moment. Truly this had been a life and death situation. What could be more important than helping to safeguard life? I was struck by the honor of working in such a field.

It was also an emotional release, as I said goodbye to the confusion and frustration I felt regarding the lack of direction in my life. The experience had rendered a death blow to my old aspirations regarding law. At the same time, I was asking forgiveness for the anger I'd felt toward God for not blessing my desires.

Although I didn't understand the Convergence Principle at the time, looking back, I can see that all three components were present. First, the experience created strong convictions regarding the importance of healthcare. Secondly, my desire to work in healthcare was stimulated. And thirdly, it dawned on me that my talents were well suited for the task.

It was certainly a defining moment, and I was stimulated to take action. I withdrew my applications to law school and fully embraced this new direction. I had no clue where it would take me, but I was excited to launch out.

It seems to me that there aren't many defining moments in life. But, we don't need many. However, defining moments and the compulsions they create are tremendously important. They determine the stage where we will perform our roles in life. They lead us to our passions.

8
Moving from Obligation to Creation

The late pastor, Charles Spurgeon, used to ask his congregation: "Do you know, dear friends, the deliciousness of work?" [149]

My defining moment marked a major change in my thinking, one that created one of the greatest blessings in my life—coming to love work more than play. That fuels passion.

Prior to that event in the operating room I had seen work as an obligation, something I had to do. Work was something that kept me from doing the things I enjoyed.

Somehow I sensed that in reality work was meant to engage me in a wondrous creative process of personal spiritual growth. Regardless of the work, it can be used to create character, to make us better people. If I would cooperate with God, every aspect of my work had the potential to make me a better person and to realize a deeper potential.

A sense of obligation is certainly not a bad thing. But to be actively cooperating with God on a daily basis in a creative process designed to lead me to a better place spiritually—now that's more fun than play. That's purposeful, passionate living.

I'll leave the subject of passion with a statement from Os Guinness:

Human beings consume and are consumed by many things— food, drink, possessions, ambition, love, to name a few. Many of these things only shrink and debase us. But in the great person and with the great cause, the consuming force may become a magnificent obsession and a heroic destiny. [150]

4
Enjoying the Fruits of Your Labor

*The Passionate Life: Experiencing
the Zeal of Christ • from Chapter Twelve*

Becoming people of passion doesn't happen overnight. It's a process. God supernaturally uses our circumstances to align three important aspects in our life experience. When those three aspects are aligned, we become people of passion. We call this the Convergence Principle. The Convergence Principle is an alignment of talents, desires and convictions.

33. In assessing your personal gifts, use the following questions to arrive at this answer: What do you do well? When people praise or compliment you, what talent or ability does it highlight? What do you enjoy doing?

I feel my gifts are:

_____

_____

34. The desires of your heart can be many things. Is there anything you feel that you need or want to accomplish before you die? If you could do anything you wanted to do, keeping in mind your abilities, what would that be?

The desires of my heart are:

_____

_____

35. As we mentioned in Chapter Seven, convictions are those core values and beliefs that we hold dear, believing they are vital to living appropriately.

My convictions are:

_____

_____

_____

36. Use the answers in Queries #33-35 to complete the following drawing. Is there an area where all three roads converge that you could consider to be your passion? (Query #37 may help you in further defining your passion.)

Author's personal example:

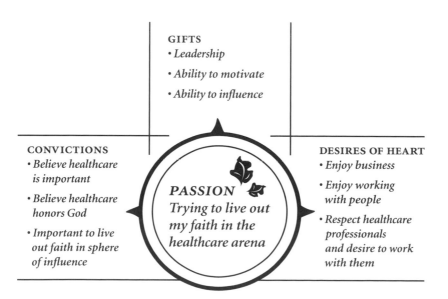

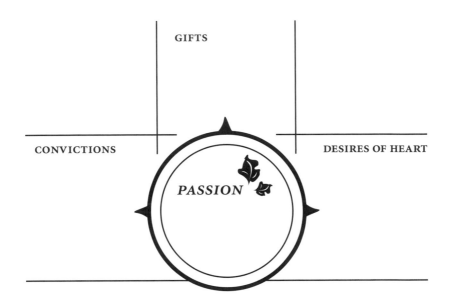

37. Convergence is often realized through a defining moment. Defining moments in turn create inner compulsions to act. These cannot be created by man. They are engineered by the sovereignty of God. Use the following to aid you in filling in the "passion" square in Query #36.

A defining moment or moments in my life have been:

_____

_____

_____

I have had the following compulsions:

_____

_____

_____

CHAPTER THIRTEEN
The Transcendent Life:
Ready for Ultimate Reality

1
Something We Take with Us When We Die

It's probably not right to love a home as much as we love ours. Thomas Jefferson said of his beloved Monticello: "I am as happy nowhere else, and in no other society, and all my wishes end, where I hope my days will, at Monticello." [151] That captures the sentiments we feel for our home, called Faranhyll, in the mountains of Colorado.

Thomas Jefferson's days did end at Monticello, on July 4, 1826— the fiftieth anniversary of the signing of the Declaration of Independence. Monticello is a place we frequent often on our pilgrimages. We end every trip there with a visit to Jefferson's burial site. It's sobering to think he was laid to rest there almost two hundred years ago.

Like Jefferson, magnificent Monticello will one day cease to exist. Ultimate reality dictates that earthly life and earthly places are temporal. With much gravity, we realize the same fate awaits us and our beloved Faranhyll.

I often sit on my porch pondering the temporal nature of life as I gaze at the beautiful mountain vistas in the distance. I always feel blessed to live at Faranhyll and am sad that I will not be able to take our home with me when I die. I wonder what will become of the place. How will my heirs deal with it? At such times, I feel the truth of this verse in Ecclesiastes:

> I am disgusted that I must leave the fruits of my hard work to others. And who can tell if my successors will be wise or foolish? And yet they will control everything I have gained by my skill and hard work. How meaningless! [152]

However, when I think about death, I am comforted by the fact that I have sincerely attempted to engage my appointments in a way that would please God. There is much I will be able to take with me. The pursuit of a relevant destiny bears fruit that is transcendent in nature.

The word transcendent is defined as above and independent of the material universe. Those things we have done with Christ, for Christ and in Christ will have eternal rewards and consequences.

2
Facing Ultimate Reality

I started this book recounting the day of my father's funeral. It seems appropriate to go full circle and end by elaborating on the events that led up to that sad day. It was one of the most profound experiences of my life.

It was November 27, 1996. My father was rushed to the hospital early that morning. I felt helpless watching him suffer, as the paramedics wheeled him to the ambulance. I wanted all the suffering to end for his sake. He had endured so much.

At the hospital, we gathered at his bedside, holding his hands, kissing him and saying our good-byes. He was a much beloved man who would soon be in God's presence forever—ultimate reality!

He was weak but coherent. Suddenly, he opened his eyes and gazed at the ceiling. At the same time, he struggled to free his hands from our grasps. Then, he feebly extended his arms upward.

He told us he loved us, and then, as he was reaching toward the ceiling, said, "I've got to go." He repeated this several times with great determination. It was as if he felt he had an important appointment to keep. Then, as his arms gently fell to his chest, he closed his eyes and was gone.

The room had a supernatural atmosphere, charged with spiritual energy. Instead of anguish, there was a sense of calm and peace. We were all mesmerized by this. I spontaneously began to pray, thanking God for Dad's life and praising Him for the rightness of the moment.

I could never communicate the spiritual intensity of those moments. But I earnestly believe that it would be impossible for a person to have been there and left the room not believing in God.

C.S. Lewis wrote in *The Great Divorce*: "There are only two kinds of people in the end: those who say to God, 'Thy will be done,' and those to whom God says, 'Thy will be done.'" [153] Therein is stated the difference between the two great eternal destinies—heaven and hell.

God docsn't send people to Hell. They send themselves there through their indifference to His love and overtures to reach into their lives. In fact Jesus tells us in the third chapter of John that He was not sent to the world to judge the world but to save it. However, He goes on to say that often people love darkness more than light.

I had a strong realization, and thankfully so, that my father had come to love The Light more than the darkness, and that he would be with God forever.

Later, commenting on the moment, our son Matt said, "After seeing what happened to Granddad, I see no reason to ever fear death." Faith was strengthened that day, not diminished.

We sensed at that moment that Dad still existed, and he'd never been better. God had tenderly called him into His presence and given us the privilege of watching. We felt the loss, but were glad that his suffering was over and rejoiced at the fact that we would see him again one day.

Wrestling with Destiny has been about dealing with our appointments in life, appointments written in pencil and ink. This was Dad's ultimate appointment, written in indelible ink. Hebrews 9:27 says:

And in as much as it is *appointed* for men to die once and after this comes the judgment. [154]

My father's dying gestures indicated that he was yearning for his appointment. I am convinced that God permitted him to see things that we could not see. It's as if He peeled back a curtain and allowed my father to gaze into the eternity that awaited him.

3
True Significance: A Life Marked by Integrity

Dad had requested that I give his eulogy. I was concerned about maintaining my composure but was determined to honor his request.

My emotions were under control up until the moment right before I had to speak. My mother had requested the singing of *The Wind Beneath My Wings*. That was a song originally sung by Bette Midler in the movie *Beaches*. The phrase, "You're my hero," is repeated often in the song. I thought of how true this was of Dad. He had spent himself on me with many acts of unconditional love.

Unfortunately, it was sung just before I was to speak. As I approached the podium, I broke down and cried uncontrollably for several minutes. Everyone knew how close we had been and how much my dad loved me. Consequently, most everyone at the funeral was soon crying as well.

Two of my closest friends rose and moved toward the podium to assist me, but I waved them off. Their gesture affected my resolve. I gathered myself and gave his eulogy with strong conviction.

Often, after we lose someone, we get a clearer picture of who they truly were. Dad's life manifested many noteworthy qualities. He was a man of excellence, a loyal friend, had a strong work ethic, and was a lover of God and family.

It wasn't what he accomplished in life that stood out. It was who he was. His life radiated integrity. It wasn't what he'd done, it was who he'd become. It was his transformed character and as a result his life influenced many characters.

Perhaps that is the great principle of destiny. It's not what we do in life that's so important. True significance lies in why we do things, in how we do them and in who we eventually become. Significant destiny is determined by who we become in Jesus Christ. And it is within our grasp to become people of integrity and Christlike character.

I'll leave you where I joined you, on the slow funeral procession up to Cemetery Hill, where I had my first brush with destiny so many years ago. We will each have a Cemetery Hill in our lives. It's my prayer that our book will help you *wrestle with your destiny.*

And I heard a voice from Heaven saying, 'Write this down: Blessed are those who die in the Lord from now on. Yes, says the Spirit, they are blessed indeed, for they shall rest from all their toils and trials; for their good deeds follow them!' [155]

4
Enjoying the Fruits of Your Labor

The Transcendent Life: Ready for
Ultimate Reality • from Chapter Thirteen

38. The word transcendent means "above and independent of the material universe." Those things we do with Christ, for Christ and in Christ will have eternal consequences.

We learn two important lessons from scripture:

Matthew 6:20 tells us to 'store up treasures in heaven.'

In Revelation we are told: '...Blessed are those who die in the Lord from now on. Yes, says the Spirit, they are blessed indeed, for they shall rest from all their toils and trials; for their good deeds follow them!' [155]

In view of my "ultimate reality" and eternity, what would I most like to be remembered for and be able to present to God when I appear before Him?

_____

_____

_____

_____

_____

_____

_____

CHAPTER FOURTEEN
Oh, Traveler

Oh, Traveler of life, tell me how will it seem
When you come to the end and reflect on the theme?

Did you capture your destiny, follow your dream?
Was your life a reflection of the Architect's scheme?

Awake, awake, prepare for the day when you must
Account for stubble and hay.

What will He look like, can His gaze you endure?
And what of life's motives? He'll question for sure.

With His appearance, terror and fright, or into
His arms, rush with delight?

The promise is there, great joy and no shame.
Fear not, fear not when comes the flame.

Simply turn your affections to the Master, I pray.
He'll guard and strengthen, illumine the way.

From the land of the dying, bound for true life,
Present a heart of true wisdom, or struggle and strife?

— Bill Williams

ACKNOWLEDGEMENTS

Endeavors are never the result of one person's efforts. I have many people to thank for helping make this one become reality. It should start with David and Jan Holder, dear friends and God's instruments, who placed trust in me and introduced me to appointments that I could never have found on my own. Without their involvement in my life, this book might never have happened.

Another friend, Monte Unger, a journalist, patiently worked with me for years, as I struggled to find "my voice."

Another journalist friend, really more of an adopted son, Robert Hornak, helped edit the book and was a source of true encouragement.

Robin Ridley did much to push the project along with her graphic design skills, as did our proof reader, Sylvia Angell. Lisa Scheideler created the interior illustrations and assisted with the layout.

Also, many thanks to Dan Coats and Jerry White who, after reviewing the manuscript, graciously wrote endorsements for us.

Our good friends, Doug and Margaret Inman, challenged my thinking and encouraged us to stay the course.

Dr. Doug Self, our pastor and friend, provided guidance along the way to make sure we didn't jump off a "theological cliff."

Thanks to our colleagues at The Pyxis Corporation whose support and devotion have been a precious part of our lives. Knowing and working with them was one of the best appointments ever.

We're indebted to our beloved sons, Mark and Matthew, who in addition to providing illustrations for us, also contributed to the book at various points along the way. This also holds true for their wives and our grandchildren, all of whom are dear to us.

Lastly, and most importantly, I am indebted to my wife Kathy— my lover, my friend and my co-laborer. Long ago we prayed for a vision for our life together. We did not want to be two people, each with separate callings in their lives, that were incidentally married. We desired one calling that was big enough for both of us, each with a part to play. This collaboration is yet another example of God's most gracious answer to that prayer.

SOURCES
Endnotes

Chapter One

1   "Above all, keep": I Peter 4:8, NASB.

2   Seneca: Quoted in Randy Alcorn, *Heaven*. Wheaton, IL: Tyndale, 2004, p. ix.

3   "valley of the shadow": Psalm 23:4, NASB.

4   "so teach us": Psalm 90:12 & 17, NASB.

5   "but I choose": John 15:16, NASB.

6   Guinness: Os Guinness, *The Call, Finding and Fulfilling the Central Purpose of Your Life*. W Publishing Group, 1998, p. 86.

7   Lamott: Anne Lamott, *Traveling Mercies, Some Thoughts on Faith*. New York: Random House, Inc., 1999, p. 75.

8   "But when it": Galatians 1:15-16, NKJ.

9   Churchill: Quoted in Richard Hough, *Winston & Clementine, The Tragedies & Triumphs of the Churchills*. New York: Bantam Books, 1991, p. 499.

10   Mark Twain: Quoted in Charles Ferguson Ball, *Heaven*. Wheaton, IL: Victor, 1980, p. 19.

11   Henrichsen: Walt Henrichsen, *Thoughts from the Diary of a Desperate Man*. El Cajon: Leadership Foundation, 1999, p. 317.

12   "So I hated": Ecclesiastes 2:17, NASB.

13   "He breathed his": Genesis 25:8, NASB.

14   "after he had": Acts 13:36, NASB.

15   "Man's steps are": Proverbs 20:24, NASB.

16   Lamott: Anne Lamott, *Bird by Bird*. New York: Anchor Books, 1995, pp. 103-104.

17   Thoreau: Henry David Thoreau, *Walden and Other Writings of Henry David Thoreau*. New York: The Modern Library, 1950, pp. 7-8.

18   "Moreover we know": Romans 8:28, J.B. Phillips.

Chapter Two

[19] Guinness: *The Call, Finding and Fulfilling the Central Purpose of Your Life*, p. 151.

[20] "For the poor": John 12:8, NASB.

[21] "In a wealthy": I Timothy 2:20, NLT.

[22] "Lamott: *Bird by Bird*, p. 18-19.

[23] "Who are Your": Acts 22:8 & 10, NLT.

[24] "Get up and": Acts 22:10b, NLT.

[25] Doctorow: Quoted in Anne Lamott, *Bird by Bird*, p. 18.

[26] "And your ears": Isaiah 30:21, NASB.

[27] "But let a": I Cor. 11:28, NASB.

[28] "I once thought": Phillipians 3:7-8, NLT.

[29] "If you try": Matthew 16:25, NLT.

[30] Jim Elliot: Quoted in Elizabeth Elliot, *Through Gates of Splendor*. Wheaton, IL: Tyndale, 1981.

[31] Chambers: Quoted in David McCaslind, *Oswald Chambers, Abandoned to God*. Grand Rapids: Discovery House Publishers, 1993, p. 51.

[32] McCaslind: *Oswald Chambers, Abandoned to God*, p. 62.

[33] "Jesus Christ came": I Timothy 1:15, NASB.

[34] Martin Luther: Quoted in Randy Alcorn, *Heaven*, p. 358.

Chapter Three

[35] "I came that": John 10:10, NASB.

[36] "In the world": John 16:33, NASB.

[37] "These things": John 16:33, NKJ.

[38] "I am leaving": John 14:27, NLT.

[39] Chesterton: Quoted in Anne Lamott, *Bird by Bird*, p. 19.

[40] Willard: Dallas Willard, *Renovation of the Heart*. Colorado Springs: NavPress, 2002, p. 134.

[41] "But now I": John 17:13, NASB.

[42] Willard: *Renovation of the Heart*, p. 132.

[43] "He who overcomes": Revelation 2:11, NASB.

[44] "He who has an ear": Revelation 2:7, NASB.

[45] "And if you": Matthew 10:42, NLT.

[46] Milne: Bruce Milne, *The Message of Heaven and Hell*. Downers Grove, IL: InterVarsity, 2002, 257.

[47] "So our aim": II Corinthians 5:9, NLT.

[48] "Behold, I am": Revelation 22:12-14, NASB.

[49] "we were gentle": I Thessalonians 2:7-8, NLT.

[50] "who is Apollos": I Corinthians 3:5-9, NLT.

[51] "bowed the knee": I Kings 19:18, NLT.

[52] "Now wherever": II Corinthians 2:14-16, NLT.

[53] Alcorn: *Heaven*, p. 28.

[54] Alcorn: *Heaven*, p. 215.

[55] "Therefore be careful": Ephesians 5:15-16, NASB.

[56] "Do not merely": Phillipians 2:5-6, NASB.

[57] "The foremost": Mark 12:29-31, NASB.

[58] "He who has": John 14:21, NASB.

[59] "And this is": John 17:3, NASB.

[60] "I know the Lord": Psalm 16:8, NLT.

Chapter Four

[61] Buechner: Frederick Buechner, *The Hungering Dark*. San Francisco: HarperSanFrancisco, 1985, p. 23.

[62] Epictetus: Epictetus, *Discourses and Enchiridion*. New York: Walter J. Black, 1944, p. 337.

[63] "Who are you": Romans 9:20-21, NASB.

[64] Tozer: A.W. Tozer, *The Knowledge of the Holy: The Attributes of God: Their Meaning in the Christian Life*. San Francisco: Harper & Row Publishers, 1961, p. 118.

[65] "I am God": Isaiah 46:9b-10, NASB.

[66] "Don't think": Esther 4:13-14, NLT.

[67] McClellan: Quoted in Geoffrey C. Ward, *The Civil War: An Illustrated History*. New York: Alfred A. Knopf, 1990, p. 71.

[68] McClellan: Quoted in Ward, *The Civil War: An Illustrated History*, p. 75.

[69] Lincoln: Quoted in Gene Smith, *Lee and Grant: A Dual Biography*. New York: New American Library, 1984, p. 135.

[70] McClellan: Quoted in Ward, *The Civil War: An Illustrated History*, pp. 110 & 112.

[71] Lincoln: Quoted in Ward, *The Civil War: An Illustrated History*, p. 90.

[72] "And Samuel said": I Samuel 13:13-14, NASB.

[73] William Jennings Bryan, etched in marble wall in the House of Representatives, U. S. Capitol.

[74] "My teaching is": John 7:16-17, NASB.

Chapter Five

[75] Kennedy: Quoted in Ralph G. Martin, *A Hero for Our Time: An Intimate Story of the Kennedy Years*. New York: MacMillan Publishing Company, 1983, p. 352.

[76] "For I know": Jeremiah 29:11, NLT.

[77] Maugham: W. Somerset Maugham, *Of Human Bondage*. Harmondsworth: Penguin Books, 1963, p. 130-131.

[78] Churchill: Winston S. Churchill, *Memoirs of the Second World War*. Boston: Houghton Mifflin Company, 1987, p. 227.

[79] Churchill: *Memoirs of the Second World War*, p. 990.

[80] Hough: *Winston and Clementine: The Triumphs and Tragedies of the Churchills*, p. 499.

[81] Churchill: Quoted in John Pearson, *The Private Lives of Winston Churchill*. New York: Simon & Schuster, 1991, p. 417.

[82] Churchill: Quoted in Pearson, *The Private Lives of Winston Churchill*, p. 418.

[83] Alcorn: *Heaven*, p. 37.

[84] Carmichael: Quoted in Frank Houghton, *Amy Carmichael of Dohnavur, The Story of a Lover and Her Beloved*. Fort Washington: Christian Literature Crusade, 1985, p. 309.

[85] Carmichael: Quoted in Elizabeth Elliot, *A Chance to Die: the Life and Legacy of Amy Carmichael*. Old Tappan: Fleming H. Revell Company, 1987, p. 372.

[86] Chambers: *My Utmost for His Highest*, March 28 reading.

[87] "For they are": Deuteronomy 32:28-29, NASB.

[88] "I will give": Isaiah 45:3.

[89] "For You light": Psalm 18:28, NKJ.

[90] "Why is it": Luke 2:49, NASB.

[91] "You are My": Mark 1:11, NLT.

[92] "My hour has": John 2:4b, NASB.

[93] "Father, the hour": John 17:1-4, NASB.

[94] "He was willing: Hebrews 12:2, NLT.

Chapter Six

[95] "May God bless": II Peter 1:2-8, NLT.

[96] "If we confess": I John 1:9, NASB.

[97] "But when He": John 16:13, NASB.

[98] "If I regard": Psalm 66:18, NKJ.

[99] "If therefore you": Matthew 5:23-24, NASB.

[100] "Pride ends in": Proverbs 29:33, NLT.

[101] "Once again you": Micah 7:19-20, NLT.

[102] "But you will": Isaiah 61:6, NASB.

[103] Lincoln: Quoted in William J. Johnson, *Abraham Lincoln the Christian*. Milford: Mott Media, 1976, p. 89.

[104] "For thus the": Acts 13:47, NASB.

[105] "And thus I": Romans 15:20, NASB.

[106] "and your ears": Isaiah 30:21, NASB.

Chapter Seven

[107] "He was teaching": Mark 1:22, NASB.

[108] "Either make the": Matthew 12:33, NASB.

[109] Chambers: *My Utmost for His Highest*, May 10 reading.

[110] Fuller: Major General J.F.C. Fuller, *Grant & Lee: A Study in Personality and Generalship*. Bloomington: Indiana University Press, 1957, pp. 111-112.

[111] Lee: Quoted in Fuller, *Grant & Lee, A Study in Personality and Generalship*, p. 111.

[112] Ann Lee: Quoted in Gene Smith, *Lee and Grant*. New York: Meiridian, 1984, p. 25.

[113] Fuller: *Grant & Lee: A Study in Personality and Generalship*, p. 102.

[114] Fuller: *Grant & Lee: A Study in Personality and Generalship*, p. 110.

[115] Lamott: Anne Lamott, *Operating Instructions, A Journal of My Son's First Year*. New York: Ballantine Books, 1993, p. 161.

[116] "Led astray from": II Corinthians 11:3b, NASB.

[117] Chambers: *My Utmost for His Highest*, September 14 reading.

[118] Chambers: *My Utmost for His Highest*, June 3 reading.

Chapter Eight

[119] "So don't worry": Matthew 6:34, NLT.

[120] "So teach us": Psalm 90:12, NASB.

[121] Kierkegaard: Søren Kierkegaard, *The Diary of Søren Kierkegaard*, pt. 5, sct. 4, no. 136 (ed. By Peter Rohde, 1960), 1843 entry.

[122] "And vast crowds": Luke 5:15-16, NLT.

[123] "And as He": Luke 19:41-44, J.B. Phillips.

[124] Tozer: A.W. Tozer, *Man: The Dwelling Place of God*. Camp Hill: Christian Publications, 1966, Chapters 21 & 24.

[125] "Let no unwholesome": Proverbs 3:27, NASB.

[126] "Do not withhold": Proverbs 3:27, NASB.

[127] Jackson: Stonewall Jackson, listed in his own copybook as his code of conduct adopted while a cadet at West Point. Stonewall Jackson House, 1984.

[128] MacDonald: Gordon MacDonald, *Ordering Your Private World*. Nashville: Oliver Nelson, 1984, p. 63.

Chapter Nine

[129] Mother Teresa: Quoted in Anne Lamott, *Operating Instructions, A Journal of My Son's First Year*, p. 243.

[130] "The grass withers": Isaiah 40:8, NLT.

[131] "I assure your": Matthew 25:45-46, NLT.

[132] Chambers: *My Utmost for His Highest*, October 18 reading.

[133] "For David, after": Acts 13:36, NASB.

Chapter Ten

[134] "the lines have": Psalm 16:6, NASB.

[135] "The Lord called": Isaiah 49:2-4, NLT.

[136] "and behold a": Matthew 3:17, NASB.

[137] Chambers: *My Utmost for His Highest*, April 18 reading.

[138] "The mind of": Proverbs 16:9, NASB.

[139] Mather: Quoted in Os Guinness, *The Call, Finding and Fulfilling the Central Purpose of Your Life*, p. 134.

[140] "O Lord my": Psalm 131:1-2, NASB.

Chapter Eleven

[141] Helm: Paul Helm, *The Last Things*. Carlisle, PA: Banner of Truth, 1989, p. 10.

[142] Alcorn: *Heaven*, p. 454.

[143] Alcorn: *Heaven*, p. 434.

[144] Chambers: *My Utmost for His Highest*, October 17 reading.

[145] Chambers: *My Utmost for His Highest*, February 19 reading.

Chapter Twelve

[146] "and to those": John 2:16-17, NASB.

[147] Guinness: *The Call, Finding and Fulfilling the Central Purpose of Your Life*, p. 46.

[148] "irresistibly drawn by": Acts 20:22, NLT.

[149] Spurgeon: Charles Spurgeon, "Foretastes of the Heavenly Life" (1857), quoted in *Spurgeon's Expository Encyclopedia*. Grand Rapids: Baker, 1951, 8:424.

[150] Guinness: *The Call, Finding and Fulfilling the Central Purpose of Your Life*, p. 79.

Chapter Thirteen

[151] Jefferson: Quoted in William Howard Adams, *Jefferson's Monticello*, Cross River Press, Ltd., 1983, frontspiece.

[152] "I am disgusted": Ecclesiastes 2:18, NLT.

[153] Lewis: C.S. Lewis, *The Great Divorce*. New York: Collier Books, MacMillan Publishing Company, 1946, pp. 72-73.

[154] "And in as ": Hebrews 9:27, NASB.

[155] "And I heard": Revelation 14:13, NLT.

Others

In addition to the specific citations above, I would like to credit the following authors for the use of their illustrations.

From Workbook Section, Chapter Two, Query #4: Adaptation of material from Lawrence J. Crabb, Jr., *Effective Biblical Counseling, A Model for Helping Caring Christians Become Capable Counselors.* Grand Rapids: The Zondervan Corporation, 1977, pp. 86-108.

From Section Three, Chapter Eight: "Railroad Illustration," from a class (1982-83) by Dr. J. Robert Clinton of Fuller Theological Seminary, Pasadena, CA. Adapted from material prepared by Fred Holland who developed materials on Theological Education by Extension.

Order additional copies of

WRESTLING WITH
DESTINY

A Layman Searches for Joy, Purpose & Fruitfulness

• • • •

To order by credit card ~ visit us on-line at **www.faranhyllpress.com**

To order by check ~ send your request plus contact information to:

> *Faranhyll* **PRESS**
> P.O. Box 2193
> Glenwood Springs, Colorado 81602
>
> Email: **authors@faranhyllpress.com**

To inquire about speaking engagements and/or contact the authors ~
please send or email your inquiries to the addresses provided above